Python 201

Intermediate Python

Michael Driscoll

Published by Michael Driscoll
Ankeny, IA

Cover art by Varya Kolesnikova

ISBN-10:0-9960628-3-1
ISBN-13:978-0-9960628-3-1

Contents

CONTENTS

Chapter 29 - The multiprocessing Module 231

Chapter 30 - The concurrent.futures Module 239

Introduction

Welcome to Python 201! This book is a sequel to my first book, **Python 101**. I wrote this book to help take you to the next level in your programming journey. It will also demonstrate to you some of the many ways you can use Python in your day-to-day work. I will be covering intermediate and some advanced level material in this book. This book is using Python 3 in all of its examples. Some of the topics covered will only work in Python 3 as some of the modules covered contain updates that were not back-ported to Python 2. Also note that this book will follow in the footsteps of my first work in that I won't be covering the topics in minute detail, but just enough to allow you to start using these building blocks yourself.

Python 201 will be split into four parts:

- Part one will cover intermediate modules
- Part two will be on a variety of topics, such as unicode, generators and iterators
- Part three will cover web related tasks with Python (but not web frameworks)
- Part four is going to cover testing code

Let me spend a few moments explaining what each part has to offer. In part one, we will cover the following intermediate modules and topics:

- argparse (Parsing command line arguments)
- collections (Replacements for Python's standard containers, such as tuple, list and dict)
- contextlib (Context Managers)
- functools (Partials, function overloading, etc)
- importing and importlib
- iterators and generators
- itertools (Creating your own iterators)
- Regular Expressions
- Type Hinting

In Part two, we will be learning what generators and iterators are as well as how they work. We'll also be looking at some of Python's special functions, like **map** and **filter**. There will be a section on Unicode, encoding and decoding strings, benchmarking and more in this section.

Part three will cover working with websites in Python. We'll look at how to browse a website with Python and scrape some data. We will work with various Python APIs to access major websites. We will use Python to create a client and a server. Finally we'll play around with Python's FTP capabilities.

Part four is all about testing your code. We will look at Python's doctest, unittest and mock modules. We'll also learn about some 3rd party packages that you can use for testing, such as tox, nose and pytest.

Please note that the chapters and sections may not all be the same length. While every topic will be covered well, not every topic will require the same page count.

About the Author

You may be wondering about who I am and why I might be knowledgeable enough about Python to write about it, so I thought I'd give you a little information about myself. I started programming in Python in the Spring of 2006 for a job. My first assignment was to port Windows login scripts from Kixtart to Python. My second project was to port VBA code (basically a GUI on top of Microsoft Office products) to Python, which is how I first got started in wxPython. I've been using Python ever since, doing a variation of backend programming and desktop front end user interfaces.

I realized that one way for me to remember how to do certain things in Python was to write about them and that's how my Python blog came about: http://www.blog.pythonlibrary.org/. As I wrote, I would receive feedback from my readers and I ended up expanding the blog to include tips, tutorials, Python news, and Python book reviews. I work regularly with Packt Publishing as a technical reviewer, which means that I get to try to check for errors in the books before they're published. I also have written for the Developer Zone (DZone) and i-programmer websites as well as the Python Software Foundation. In November 2013, DZone published **The Essential Core Python Cheat Sheet** that I co-authored. I have also self-published Python 101, which came out in June 2014.

Conventions

As with most technical books, this one includes a few conventions that you need to be aware of. New topics and terminology will be in **bold**. You will also see some examples that look like the following:

```
1   >>> myString = "Welcome to Python!"
```

The >>> is a Python prompt symbol. You will see this in the Python **interpreter** and in **IDLE**. Other code examples will be shown in a similar manner, but without the >>>.

Requirements

You will need a working **Python 3** installation. Most Linux and Mac machines come with Python already installed, however they might not have Python 3 as their default. If you happen to find yourself without Python, you can go download a copy from http://python.org/download/[1]. There are up-to-date installation instructions on their website, so I won't include any installation instructions in this book. Any additional requirements will be explained later on in the book.

Reader Feedback

I welcome feedback about my writings. If you'd like to let me know what you thought of the book, you can send comments to the following address:

comments@pythonlibrary.org

Errata

I try my best not to publish errors in my writings, but it happens from time to time. If you happen to see an error in this book, feel free to let me know by emailing me at the following:

errata@pythonlibrary.org

Now let's get started!

---

[1] http://python.org/download/

Part I - The Intermediate Modules

Welcome to part I. In this section of the book, we will be looking at a sampling of some of Python's intermediate level modules and concepts. There are two big topics that will be covered plus eight chapters devoted to specific modules from the Python Standard Library. For the first topical chapter, you will learn about how iterators and generators work and what the differences are between the two of them. In the second, you will learn all about how Python's importing system works.

Here's a more specific run-down of what's covered in this section:

- Chapter 1 - The argparse module
- Chapter 2 - The collections module
- Chapter 3 - The contextlib module (Context Managers)
- Chapter 4 - The functools module (Function overloading, caching, etc)
- Chapter 5 - All about imports
- Chapter 6 - The importlib module
- Chapter 7 - Iterators and Generators
- Chapter 8 - The itertools module
- Chapter 9 - The re module (An Intro to Regex in Python)
- Chapter 10 - The typing module (Type Hinting)

Let's get started!

Chapter 1 - An Intro to Argument Parsing using argparse

Have you ever wondered how to process command line arguments in Python? Yeah, there's a module for that. It's called argparse, which is a replacement for optparse. In this article, we'll be taking a whirlwind tour of this helpful module. Let's start with something simple!

Getting Started

I have always found the simplest way to explain a coding concept is to show some code. So that's what we're going to do. Here's a super simple example that doesn't do much of anything:

```
1  >>> import argparse
2  >>> parser = argparse.ArgumentParser(
3  ...         description="A simple argument parser",
4  ...         epilog="This is where you might put example usage"
5  ...     )
6  ...
7  >>> parser.print_help()
8  usage: _sandbox.py [-h]
9
10 A simple argument parser
11
12 optional arguments:
13   -h, --help  show this help message and exit
14
15 This is where you might put example usage
```

Here we just import argparse and give it a description and set up a usage section. The idea here is that when you ask the program you are creating for help, it will tell you how to use it. In this case, it prints out a simple description, the default optional arguments ("-h" in this case) and example usage.

Now let's make this example a bit more concrete. You won't normally be parsing arguments from the command-line after all. So we'll move the code into a Python function inside of a Python file:

```
1   # arg_demo.py
2
3   import argparse
4
5
6   def get_args():
7       """"""
8       parser = argparse.ArgumentParser(
9           description="A simple argument parser",
10          epilog="This is where you might put example usage"
11      )
12      return parser.parse_args()
13
14  if __name__ == '__main__':
15      get_args()
```

Now let's call the script from the command line:

```
1   python arg_demo.py -h
```

This will print out the help text like we saw earlier. Now let's learn about how to add some of our own custom arguments.

Adding Arguments

Let's write some code that adds three new arguments that our parser can understand. We'll add an argument that is required and two that are not. We'll also look at adding a default and a required type. Here's the code:

```
1   # arg_demo2.py
2
3   import argparse
4
5
6   def get_args():
7       """"""
8       parser = argparse.ArgumentParser(
9           description="A simple argument parser",
10          epilog="This is where you might put example usage"
11      )
12
```

```
13          # required argument
14          parser.add_argument('-x', action="store", required=True,
15                              help='Help text for option X')
16          # optional arguments
17          parser.add_argument('-y', help='Help text for option Y', default=False)
18          parser.add_argument('-z', help='Help text for option Z', type=int)
19          print(parser.parse_args())
20
21      if __name__ == '__main__':
22          get_args()
```

Now let's run it a few times so you can see what happens:

```
1   mike@pc:~/py/argsparsing$ python arg_demo2.py
2   usage: arg_demo2.py [-h] -x X [-y Y] [-z Z]
3   arg_demo2.py: error: argument -x is required
4
5   mike@pc:~/py/argsparsing$ python arg_demo2.py -x something
6   Namespace(x='something', y=False, z=None)
7
8   mike@pc:~/py/argsparsing$ python arg_demo2.py -x something -y text
9   Namespace(x='something', y='text', z=None)
10
11  mike@pc:~/py/argsparsing$ python arg_demo2.py -x something -z text
12  usage: arg_demo2.py [-h] -x X [-y Y] [-z Z]
13  arg_demo2.py: error: argument -z: invalid int value: 'text'
14
15  mike@pc:~/py/argsparsing$ python arg_demo2.py -x something -z 10
16  Namespace(x='something', y=False, z=10)
```

As you can see, if you run the code without passing it any arguments, you will get an error. Next we pass it just the required argument so you can see what the defaults are for the other two. Then we try passing "text" to the '-y' argument and that gets stored, so we know it doesn't require a Boolean. The last two examples show what happens when you pass an invalid and a valid value to the '-z' argument.

By the way, the argument names do not have to be one character in length. You can change those something more descriptive, like 'arg1' or 'simulator' or whatever you want.

Short Options and Long Options

Let's take a look at how we might use a short option versus a long a one. We actually are already using the short option here:

```
1    parser.add_argument('-x', action="store", required=True,
2                        help='Help text for option X')
```

If we wanted a long option, then we'd just need to add it right after the short one. Here's an example:

```
1    parser.add_argument('-x', '--execute', action="store", required=True,
2                        help='Help text for option X')
```

You will note that a long option is more than one character in length and that it must start with two dashes instead of one.

Options that Conflict

What do you do if you have options that conflict with each other? A common example would be running your application in verbose mode versus quiet mode. You can run it in either mode, but not both. How do we prevent the user from running it that way though? It's actually quite easy via the **mutually_exclusive_group** function. Let's pretend that options **x** and **y** cannot run at the same time and modify our code accordingly:

```
1    import argparse
2
3
4    def get_args():
5        """"""
6        parser = argparse.ArgumentParser(
7            description="A simple argument parser",
8            epilog="This is where you might put example usage"
9        )
10
11       group = parser.add_mutually_exclusive_group()
12       group.add_argument('-x', '--execute', action="store",
13                          help='Help text for option X')
14       group.add_argument('-y', help='Help text for option Y', default=False)
15
16       parser.add_argument('-z', help='Help text for option Z', type=int)
17       print(parser.parse_args())
18
19   if __name__ == '__main__':
20       get_args()
```

You will note that we have to create a mutually exclusive group. Then we add the options that need to be mutually exclusive to that group. The rest go into the regular parser group. Let's try running the code with both options like this:

```
1   python arg_demo3.py -x 10 -y 2
```

When I did this command, I ended up getting the following output:

```
1   usage: arg_demo3.py [-h] [-x EXECUTE | -y Y] [-z Z]
2   arg_demo2.py: error: argument -y: not allowed with argument -x/--execute
```

Obviously that didn't work and the argparse module told us why.

Wrapping Up

You now know how to create the basics of an argument parser. There are many other aspects of this module that you might be interested in, such as defining an alternate destination name for the argument to be saved to, using different prefixes (i.e. '+' instead of '-'), creating argument groups and more. I recommend checking out the documentation for more details.

Chapter 2 - The collections module

Python's collections module has specialized container datatypes that can be used to replace Python's general purpose containers (dict, tuple, list, and set). We will be studying the following parts of this fun module:

- ChainMap
- defaultdict
- deque
- namedtuple
- OrderedDict

There is a sub-module of collections called abc or Abstract Base Classes. These will not be covered in this chapter.

Let's get started with the ChainMap container!

ChainMap

A **ChainMap** is a class that provides the ability to link multiple mappings together such that they end up being a single unit. If you look at the documentation, you will notice that it accepts **maps**, which means that a ChainMap will accept any number of mappings or dictionaries and turn them into a single view that you can update. Let's look at an example so you can see how this works:

```
1  >>> from collections import ChainMap
2  >>> car_parts = {'hood': 500, 'engine': 5000, 'front_door': 750}
3  >>> car_options = {'A/C': 1000, 'Turbo': 2500, 'rollbar': 300}
4  >>> car_accessories = {'cover': 100, 'hood_ornament': 150, 'seat_cover': 99}
5  >>> car_pricing = ChainMap(car_accessories, car_options, car_parts)
6  >>> car_pricing['hood']
7  500
```

Here we import **ChainMap** from our collections module. Next we create three dictionaries. Then we create an instance of our ChainMap by passing in the three dictionaries that we just created.

Finally, we try accessing one of the keys in our ChainMap. When we do this, the ChainMap will go through each map in order to see if that key exists and has a value. If it does, then the ChainMap will return the first value it finds that matches that key.

This is especially useful if you want to set up defaults. Let's pretend that we want to create an application that has some defaults. The application will also be aware of the operating system's environment variables. If there is an environment variable that matches one of the keys that we are defaulting to in our application, the the environment will override our default. Let's further pretend that we can pass arguments to our application. These arguments take precendence over the environment and the defaults. This is one place where a ChainMap can really shine. Let's look at a simple example that's based on one from Python's documentation:

```python
import argparse
import os

from collections import ChainMap


def main():
    app_defaults = {'username':'admin', 'password':'admin'}

    parser = argparse.ArgumentParser()
    parser.add_argument('-u', '--username')
    parser.add_argument('-p', '--password')
    args = parser.parse_args()
    command_line_arguments = {key:value for key, value
                                in vars(args).items() if value}

    chain = ChainMap(command_line_arguments, os.environ,
                     app_defaults)
    print(chain['username'])

if __name__ == '__main__':
    main()
    os.environ['username'] = 'test'
    main()
```

Let's break this down a little. Here we import Python's **argparse** module along with the **os** module. We also import ChainMap.Next we have a simple function that has some silly defaults. I've seen these defaults used for some popular routers. Then we set up our argument parser and tell it how to handle certain command line options. You will notice that argparse doesn't provide a way to get a dictionary object of its arguments, so we use a dict comprehension to extract what we need. The other cool piece here is the use of Python's built-in **vars**. If you were to call it without an argument, vars would behave like Python's built-in **locals**. But if you do pass in an object, then vars is the equivalent to object's **__dict__** property.

In other words, **vars(args)** equals **args.__dict__**. Finally create our ChainMap by passing in our command line arguments (if there are any), then the environment variables and finally the defaults. At the end of the code, we try calling our function, then setting an environment variable and calling it again. Give it a try and you'll see that it prints out **admin** and then **test** as expected. Now let's try calling the script with a command line argument:

```
1  python chain_map.py -u mike
```

When I ran this, I got **mike** back twice. This is because our command line argument overrides everything else. It doesn't matter that we set the environment because our ChainMap will look at the command line arguments first before anything else.

Now that you know how to use ChainMaps, we can move on to the Counter!

Counter

The collections module also provides us with a neat little tool that supports convenient and fast tallies. This tool is called **Counter**. You can run it against most iterables. Let's try it out with a string!

```
1  >>> from collections import Counter
2  >>> Counter('superfluous')
3  Counter({'u': 3, 's': 2, 'e': 1, 'l': 1, 'f': 1, 'o': 1, 'r': 1, 'p': 1})
4  >>> counter = Counter('superfluous')
5  >>> counter['u']
6  3
```

In this example, we import **Counter** from collections and then pass it a string. This returns a Counter object that is a subclass of Python's dictionary. We then run the same command but assign it to the variable **counter** so we can access the dictionary a bit easier. In this case, we saw that the letter "u" occurs three times in the example string.

The Counter provides a few methods that might interest you. For example, you can call **elements** which will an iterator over the elements that are in the dictionary, but in an arbitrary order. You can kind of think of this function as a "scrambler" as the output in this case is a scrambled version of the string.

```
1  >>> list(counter.elements())
2  ['e', 'l', 'f', 'o', 'r', 's', 's', 'p', 'u', 'u', 'u']
```

Another useful method is **most_common**. You can ask the Counter what the most common items are by passing in a number that represents what the top recurring "n" items are:

```
1  >>> counter.most_common(2)
2  [('u', 3), ('s', 2)]
```

Here we just ask our Counter what the top two most recurring items were. As you can see, it produced a list of tuples that tells us "u" occurred 3 times and "s" occurred twice.

The other method that I want to cover is the **subtract** method. The subtract method accepts an iterable or a mapping and the uses that argument to subtract. It's a bit easier to explain if you see some code:

```
1  >>> counter_one = Counter('superfluous')
2  >>> counter_one
3  Counter({'u': 3, 's': 2, 'e': 1, 'l': 1, 'f': 1, 'o': 1, 'r': 1, 'p': 1})
4  >>> counter_two = Counter('super')
5  >>> counter_one.subtract(counter_two)
6  None
7  >>> counter_one
8  Counter({'u': 2, 'l': 1, 'f': 1, 'o': 1, 's': 1, 'e': 0, 'r': 0, 'p': 0})
```

So here we recreate our first counter and print it out so we know what's in it. That we create our second Counter object. Finally we subtract the second counter from the first. If you look carefully at the output at the end, you will notice the that number of letters for five of the items has been decremented by one.

As I mentioned at the beginning of this section, you can use the Counter against any iterable or mapping, so you don't have to just use strings. You can also pass it tuples, dictionaries and lists! Give it a try on your own to see how it works with those other data types.

Now we're ready to move on to the defaultdict!

defaultdict

The collections module has a handy tool called **defaultdict**. The defaultdict is a subclass of Python's **dict** that accepts a default_factory as its primary argument. The default_factory is usually a Python type, such as int or list, but you can also use a function or a lambda too. Let's start by creating a regular Python dictionary that counts the number of times each word is used in a sentence:

```
1  sentence = "The red for jumped over the fence and ran to the zoo for food"
2  words = sentence.split(' ')
3
4  reg_dict = {}
5  for word in words:
6      if word in reg_dict:
7          reg_dict[word] += 1
8      else:
9          reg_dict[word] = 1
10
11 print(reg_dict)
```

If you run this code, you should see output that is similar to the following:

```
1  {'The': 1,
2   'and': 1,
3   'fence': 1,
4   'food': 1,
5   'for': 2,
6   'jumped': 1,
7   'over': 1,
8   'ran': 1,
9   'red': 1,
10  'the': 2,
11  'to': 1,
12  'zoo': 1}
```

Now let's try doing the same thing with defaultdict!

```
1  from collections import defaultdict
2
3
4  sentence = "The red for jumped over the fence and ran to the zoo for food"
5  words = sentence.split(' ')
6
7  d = defaultdict(int)
8  for word in words:
9      d[word] += 1
10
11 print(d)
```

You will notice right away that the code is much simpler. The defaultdict will automatically assign zero as the value to any key it doesn't already have in it. We add one so it makes more sense and it will also increment if the word appears multiple times in the sentence.

```
 1  defaultdict(<class 'int'>,
 2              {'The': 1,
 3               'and': 1,
 4               'fence': 1,
 5               'food': 1,
 6               'for': 2,
 7               'jumped': 1,
 8               'over': 1,
 9               'ran': 1,
10               'red': 1,
11               'the': 2,
12               'to': 1,
13               'zoo': 1})
```

Now let's try using a Python list type as our default factory. We'll start off with a regular dictionary first, as before.

```
 1  my_list = [(1234, 100.23), (345, 10.45), (1234, 75.00),
 2             (345, 222.66), (678, 300.25), (1234, 35.67)]
 3
 4  reg_dict = {}
 5  for acct_num, value in my_list:
 6      if acct_num in reg_dict:
 7          reg_dict[acct_num].append(value)
 8      else:
 9          reg_dict[acct_num] = [value]
10
11  print(reg_dict)
```

This example is based on some code I wrote a few years ago. Basically I was reading a file line by line and needed to grab the account number and the payment amount and keep track of them. Then at the end, I would sum up each account. We're skipping the summing part here. If You run this code, you should get some output similar to the following:

```
 1  {345: [10.45, 222.66], 678: [300.25], 1234: [100.23, 75.0, 35.67]}
```

Now let's re-implement this code using defaultdict:

```
 1  from collections import defaultdict
 2
 3
 4  my_list = [(1234, 100.23), (345, 10.45), (1234, 75.00),
 5             (345, 222.66), (678, 300.25), (1234, 35.67)]
 6
 7  d = defaultdict(list)
 8  for acct_num, value in my_list:
 9      d[acct_num].append(value)
10
11  print(d)
```

Once again, this cuts out the if/else conditional logic and makes the code easier to follow. Here's the output from the code above:

```
 1  defaultdict(<class 'list'>,
 2              {345: [10.45, 222.66],
 3               678: [300.25],
 4               1234: [100.23, 75.0, 35.67]})
```

This is some pretty cool stuff! Let's go ahead and try using a lambda too as our default_factory!

```
 1  >>> from collections import defaultdict
 2  >>> animal = defaultdict(lambda: "Monkey")
 3  >>> animal['Sam'] = 'Tiger'
 4  >>> print (animal['Nick'])
 5  Monkey
 6  >>> animal
 7  defaultdict(<function <lambda> at 0x7f32f26da8c0>, {'Nick': 'Monkey', 'Sam': 'Ti\
 8  ger'})
```

Here we create a defaultdict that will assign 'Monkey' as the default value to any key. The first key we set to 'Tiger', then the next key we don't set at all. If you print the second key, you will see that it got assigned 'Monkey'. In case you haven't noticed yet, it's basically impossible to cause a KeyError to happen as long as you set the default_factory to something that makes sense. The documentation does mention that if you happen to set the default_factory to None, then you will receive a KeyError. Let's see how that works:

```
1  >>> from collections import defaultdict
2  >>> x = defaultdict(None)
3  >>> x['Mike']
4  Traceback (most recent call last):
5    Python Shell, prompt 41, line 1
6  KeyError: 'Mike'
```

In this case, we just created a very broken defaultdict. It can no longer assign a default to our key, so it throws a KeyError instead. Of course, since it is a subclass of dict, we can just set the key to some value and it will work. But that kind of defeats the purpose of the defaultdict.

deque

According to the Python documentation, **deques** "are a generalization of stacks and queues". They are pronounced "deck" which is short for "double-ended queue". They are a replacement container for the Python list. Deques are thread-safe and support memory efficient appends and pops from either side of the deque. A list is optimized for fast fixed-length operations. You can get all the gory details in the Python documentation. A deque accepts a **maxlen** argument which sets the bounds for the deque. Otherwise the deque will grow to an arbitrary size. When a bounded deque is full, any new items added will cause the same number of items to be popped off the other end.

As a general rule, if you need fast appends or fast pops, use a deque. If you need fast random access, use a list. Let's take a few moments to look at how you might create and use a deque.

```
1  >>> from collections import deque
2  >>> import string
3  >>> d = deque(string.ascii_lowercase)
4  >>> for letter in d:
5  ...      print(letter)
```

Here we import the deque from our collections module and we also import the **string** module. To actually create an instance of a deque, we need to pass it an iterable. In this case, we passed it **string.ascii_lowercase**, which returns a list of all the lower case letters in the alphabet. Finally, we loop over our deque and print out each item. Now let's look at at a few of the methods that deque possesses.

```
1  >>> d.append('bork')
2  >>> d
3  deque(['a', 'b', 'c', 'd', 'e', 'f', 'g', 'h', 'i', 'j', 'k', 'l', 'm', 'n',
4         'o', 'p', 'q', 'r', 's', 't', 'u', 'v', 'w', 'x', 'y', 'z', 'bork'])
5  >>> d.appendleft('test')
6  >>> d
7  deque(['test', 'a', 'b', 'c', 'd', 'e', 'f', 'g', 'h', 'i', 'j', 'k', 'l', 'm',
8         'n', 'o', 'p', 'q', 'r', 's', 't', 'u', 'v', 'w', 'x', 'y', 'z', 'bork'])
9  >>> d.rotate(1)
10 >>> d
11 deque(['bork', 'test', 'a', 'b', 'c', 'd', 'e', 'f', 'g', 'h', 'i', 'j', 'k', 'l\
12 ',
13        'm', 'n', 'o', 'p', 'q', 'r', 's', 't', 'u', 'v', 'w', 'x', 'y', 'z'])
```

Let's break this down a bit. First we append a string to the right end of the deque. Then we append another string to the left side of the deque.. Lastly, we call **rotate** on our deque and pass it a one, which causes it to rotate one time to the right. In other words, it causes one item to rotate off the right end and onto the front. You can pass it a negative number to make the deque rotate to the left instead.

Let's finish out this section by looking at an example that's based on something from the Python documentation:

```python
1  from collections import deque
2
3
4  def get_last(filename, n=5):
5      """
6      Returns the last n lines from the file
7      """
8      try:
9          with open(filename) as f:
10             return deque(f, n)
11     except OSError:
12         print("Error opening file: {}".format(filename))
13         raise
```

This code works in much the same way as Linux's **tail** program does. Here we pass in a filename to our script along with the n number of lines we want returned. The deque is bounded to whatever number we pass in as n. This means that once the deque is full, when new lines are read in and added to the deque, older lines are popped off the other end and discarded. I also wrapped the file opening **with** statement in a simple exception handler because it's really easy to pass in a malformed path. This will catch files that don't exist for example.

Now we're ready to move on and learn about the namedtuple.

namedtuple

The one that we'll be focusing on in this section is the **namedtuple** which you can use to replace Python's **tuple**. Of course, the namedtuple is not a drop-in replacement as you will soon see. I have seen some programmers use it like a struct. If you haven't used a language with a struct in it, then that needs a little explanation. A struct is basically a complex data type that groups a list of variables under one name. Let's look at an example of how to create a namedtuple so you can see how they work:

```
1  from collections import namedtuple
2
3  Parts = namedtuple('Parts', 'id_num desc cost amount')
4  auto_parts = Parts(id_num='1234', desc='Ford Engine',
5                     cost=1200.00, amount=10)
6  print(auto_parts.id_num)
```

Here we import **namedtuple** from the **collections** module. Then we called namedtuple, which will return a new subclass of a tuple but with named fields. So basically we just created a new tuple class. you will note that we have a strange string as our second argument. This is a space delimited list of properties that we want to create.

Now that we have our shiny new class, let's create an instance of it! As you can see above, we do that as our very next step when we create the **auto_parts** object. Now we can access the various items in our auto_parts using dot notation because they are now properties of our Parts class.

One of the benefits of using a namedtuple over a regular tuple is that you no longer have to keep track of each item's index because now each item is named and accessed via a class property. Here's the difference in code:

```
1  >>> auto_parts = ('1234', 'Ford Engine', 1200.00, 10)
2  >>> auto_parts[2]  # access the cost
3  1200.0
4  >>> id_num, desc, cost, amount = auto_parts
5  >>> id_num
6  '1234'
```

In the code above, we create a regular tuple and access the cost of the vehicle engine by telling Python the appropriate index we want. Alternatively, we can also extract everything from the tuple using multiple assignment. Personally, I prefer the namedtuple approach just because it fits the mind easier and you can use Python's **dir()** method to inspect the tuple and find out its properties. Give that a try and see what happens!

The other day I was looking for a way to convert a Python dictionary into an object and I came across some code that did something like this:

```
1  >>> from collections import namedtuple
2
3  >>> Parts = {'id_num':'1234', 'desc':'Ford Engine',
4          'cost':1200.00, 'amount':10}
5  >>> parts = namedtuple('Parts', Parts.keys())(**Parts)
6  >>> parts
7  Parts(amount=10, cost=1200.0, id_num='1234', desc='Ford Engine')
```

This is some weird code, so let's take it a piece at a time. The first line we import namedtuple as before. Next we create a Parts dictionary. So far, so good. Now we're ready for the weird part. Here we create our namedtuple class and name it 'Parts'. The second argument is a list of the keys from our dictionary. The last piece is this strange piece of code: (Parts)**. The double asterisk means that we are calling our class using keyword arguments, which in this case is our dictionary. We could split this line into two parts to make it a little clearer:

```
1  >>> parts = namedtuple('Parts', Parts.keys())
2  >>> parts
3  <class '__main__.Parts'>
4  >>> auto_parts = parts(**Parts)
5  >>> auto_parts
6  Parts(amount=10, cost=1200.0, id_num='1234', desc='Ford Engine')
```

So here we do the same thing as before, except that we create the class first, then we call the class with our dictionary to create an object. The only other piece I want to mention is that namedtuple also accepts a **verbose** argument and a **rename** argument. The verbose argument is a flag that will print out class definition right before it's built if you set it to True. The rename argument is useful if you're creating your namedtuple from a database or some other system that your program doesn't control as it will automatically rename the properties for you.

At this point you should be familiar enough with the namedtuple to use it yourself, so let's check out the OrderedDict!

OrderedDict

Python's collections module has another great subclass of dict known as **OrderedDict**. As the name implies, this dictionary keeps track of the order of the keys as they are added. If you create a regular dict, you will note that it is an unordered data collection:

```
1  >>> d = {'banana': 3, 'apple':4, 'pear': 1, 'orange': 2}
2  >>> d
3  {'apple': 4, 'banana': 3, 'orange': 2, 'pear': 1}
```

Every time you print it out, the order may be different. There are times when you will need to loop over the keys of your dictionary in a specific order. For example, I have had a use case where I needed the keys sorted so I could loop over them in order. To do that, you can do the following:

```
1  >>> keys = d.keys()
2  >>> keys
3  dict_keys(['apple', 'orange', 'banana', 'pear'])
4  >>> keys = sorted(keys)
5  ['apple', 'banana', 'orange', 'pear']
6  >>> for key in keys:
7  ...     print (key, d[key])
8  ...
9  apple 4
10 banana 3
11 orange 2
12 pear 1
```

Let's create an instance of an OrderedDict using our original dict, but during the creation, we'll sort the dictionary's keys:

```
1  >>> from collections import OrderedDict
2  >>> d = {'banana': 3, 'apple':4, 'pear': 1, 'orange': 2}
3  >>> new_d = OrderedDict(sorted(d.items()))
4  >>> new_d
5  OrderedDict([('apple', 4), ('banana', 3), ('orange', 2), ('pear', 1)])
6  >>> for key in new_d:
7  ...     print (key, new_d[key])
8  ...
9  apple 4
10 banana 3
11 orange 2
12 pear 1
```

Here we create our OrderedDict by sorting it on the fly using Python's sorted built-in function. The sorted function takes in the dictionary's items, which is a list of tuples that represent the key pairs of the dictionary. It sorts them and then passes them into the OrderedDict, which will retain their order. Thus when we go to print our the keys and values, they are in the order we expect. If you were to loop over a regular dictionary (not a sorted list of keys), the order would change all the time.

Note that if you add new keys, they will be added to the end of the OrderedDict instead of being automatically sorted.

Something else to note about OrderDicts is that when you go to compare two OrderedDicts, they will not only test the items for equality, but also that the order is correct. A regular dictionary only looks at the contents of the dictionary and doesn't care about its order.

Finally, OrderDicts have two new methods in Python 3: popitem and move_to_end. The popitem method will return and remove a (key, item) pair. The move_to_end method will move an existing key to either end of the OrderedDict. The item will be moved right end if the last argument for OrderedDict is set to True (which is the default), or to the beginning if it is False.

Interestingly, OrderedDicts support reverse iteration using Python's reversed built-in function:

```
1  >>> for key in reversed(new_d):
2  ...      print (key, new_d[key])
3  ...
4  pear 1
5  orange 2
6  banana 3
7  apple 4
```

Pretty neat, although you probably won't be needing that functionality every day.

Wrapping Up

We've covered a lot of ground in this chapter. You learned how to use a defaultdict and an OrderedDict. We also learned about a neat subclass of Python's list, the deque. Finally we looked at how to use a namedtuple to do various activities. I hope you found each of these collections interesting. They may be of great use to you in your own coding life.

Chapter 3 - Context Managers

Python came out with a special new keyword several years ago in Python 2.5 that is known as the **with statement**. This new keyword allows a developer to create context managers. But wait! What's a context manager? They are handy constructs that allow you to set something up and tear something down automatically. For example, you might want to open a file, write a bunch of stuff to it and then close it. This is probably the classic example of a context manager. In fact, Python creates one automatically for you when you open a file using the **with statement**:

```
1  with open(path, 'w') as f_obj:
2      f_obj.write(some_data)
```

Back in Python 2.4, you would have to do it the old fashioned way:

```
1  f_obj = open(path, 'w')
2  f_obj.write(some_data)
3  f_obj.close()
```

The way this works under the covers is by using some of Python's magic methods: **__enter__** and **__exit__**. Let's try creating our own context manager to demonstrate how this all works!

Creating a Context Manager class

Rather than rewrite Python's open method here, we'll create a context manager that can create a SQLite database connection and close it when it's done. Here's a simple example:

```
1   import sqlite3
2
3
4   class DataConn:
5       """"""
6
7       def __init__(self, db_name):
8           """Constructor"""
9           self.db_name = db_name
10
11      def __enter__(self):
12          """
13          Open the database connection
14          """
15          self.conn = sqlite3.connect(self.db_name)
16          return self.conn
17
18      def __exit__(self, exc_type, exc_val, exc_tb):
19          """
20          Close the connection
21          """
22          self.conn.close()
23          if exc_val:
24              raise
25
26  if __name__ == '__main__':
27      db = '/home/mdriscoll/test.db'
28      with DataConn(db) as conn:
29          cursor = conn.cursor()
```

In the code above, we created a class that takes a path to a SQLite database file. The __enter__ method executes automatically where it creates and returns the database connection object. Now that we have that, we can create a cursor and write to the database or query it. When we exit the with statement, it causes the __exit__ method to execute and that closes the connection.

Let's try creating a context manager using another method.

Creating a Context Manager using contextlib

Python 2.5 not only added the with statement, but it also added the contextlib module. This allows us to create a context manager using contextlib's contextmanager function as a decorator. Let's try creating a context manager that opens and closes a file after all:

```
1   from contextlib import contextmanager
2
3   @contextmanager
4   def file_open(path):
5       try:
6           f_obj = open(path, 'w')
7           yield f_obj
8       except OSError:
9           print("We had an error!")
10      finally:
11          print('Closing file')
12          f_obj.close()
13
14  if __name__ == '__main__':
15      with file_open('/home/mdriscoll/test.txt') as fobj:
16          fobj.write('Testing context managers')
```

Here we just import **contextmanager** from **contextlib** and decorate our file_open function with it. This allows us to call file_open using Python's with statement. In our function, we open the file and then yield it out so the calling function can use it.

Once the **with** statement ends, control returns back to the file_open function and it continues with the code following the yield statement. That causes the finally statement to execute, which closes the file. If we happen to have an **OSError** while working with the file, it gets caught and finally statement still closes the file handler.

contextlib.closing(thing)

The contextlib module comes with some other handy utilities. The first one is the **closing** class which will close the thing upon the completion of code block. The Python documentation gives an example that's similar to the following one:

```
1   from contextlib import contextmanager
2
3   @contextmanager
4   def closing(db):
5       try:
6           yield db.conn()
7       finally:
8           db.close()
```

Basically what we're doing is creating a closing function that's wrapped in a contextmanager. This is the equivalent of what the closing class does. The difference is that instead of a decorator, we can use the **closing** class itself in our with statement. Let's take a look:

```
1    from contextlib import closing
2    from urllib.request import urlopen
3
4    with closing(urlopen('http://www.google.com')) as webpage:
5        for line in webpage:
6            # process the line
7            pass
```

In this example, we open a url page but wrap it with our closing class. This will cause the handle to the web page to be closed once we fall out of the with statement's code block.

contextlib.suppress(*exceptions)

Another handy little tool is the **suppress** class which was added in Python 3.4. The idea behind this context manager utility is that it can suppress any number of exceptions. Let's say we want to ignore the **FileNotFoundError** exception. If you were to write the following context manager, it wouldn't work:

```
1    >>> with open('fauxfile.txt') as fobj:
2            for line in fobj:
3                print(line)
4
5    Traceback (most recent call last):
6      Python Shell, prompt 4, line 1
7    builtins.FileNotFoundError: [Errno 2] No such file or directory: 'fauxfile.txt'
```

As you can see, this context manager doesn't handle this exception. If you want to ignore this error, then you can do the following:

```
1    from contextlib import suppress
2
3    with suppress(FileNotFoundError):
4        with open('fauxfile.txt') as fobj:
5            for line in fobj:
6                print(line)
```

Here we import **suppress** and pass it the exception that we want to ignore, which in this case is the FileNotFoundError exception. If you run this code, you will note that nothing happens as the file does not exist, but an error is also not raised. It should be noted that this context manager is **reentrant**. This will be explained later on in this section.

contextlib.redirect_stdout / redirect_stderr

The contextlib library has a couple of neat tools for redirecting stdout and stderr that were added in Python 3.4 and 3.5 respectively. Before these tools were added, if you wanted to redirect stdout, you would do something like this:

```python
path = '/path/to/text.txt'

with open(path, 'w') as fobj:
    sys.stdout = fobj
    help(sum)
```

With the contextlib module, you can now do the following:

```python
from contextlib import redirect_stdout

path = '/path/to/text.txt'
with open(path, 'w') as fobj:
    with redirect_stdout(fobj):
        help(redirect_stdout)
```

In both of these examples, we are redirecting stdout to a file. When we call Python's **help**, instead of printing to stdout, it gets saved directly to the file. You could also redirect stdout to some kind of buffer or a text control type widget from a user interface toolkit like Tkinter or wxPython.

ExitStack

ExitStack is a context manager that will allow you to easily programmatically combine other context managers and cleanup functions. It sounds kind of confusing at first, so let's take a look at an example from the Python documentation to help us understand this idea a bit better:

```python
>>> from contextlib import ExitStack
>>> with ExitStack as stack:
        file_objects = [stack.enter_context(open(filename))
            for filename in filenames]
                ]
```

This code basically creates a series of context managers inside the list comprehension. The ExitStack maintains a stack of registered callbacks that it will call in reverse order when the instance it closed, which happens when we exit the the bottom of the **with** statement.

There are a bunch of neat examples in the Python documentation for contextlib where you can learn about topics like the following:

- Catching exceptions from __enter__ methods
- Supports a variable number of context managers
- Replacing any use of try-finally
- and much more!

I highly recommend checking it out so you get a good feel for how powerful this class is.

Reentrant Context Managers

Most context managers that you create will be written such that they can only be used once using a **with** statement. Here's a simple example:

```
1  >>> from contextlib import contextmanager
2  >>> @contextmanager
3  ... def single():
4  ...     print('Yielding')
5  ...     yield
6  ...     print('Exiting context manager')
7  >>> context = single()
8  >>> with context:
9  ...     pass
10 ...
11 Yielding
12 Exiting context manager
13 >>> with context:
14 ...     pass
15 ...
16 Traceback (most recent call last):
17   Python Shell, prompt 9, line 1
18   File "/usr/local/lib/python3.5/contextlib.py", line 61, in __enter__
19     raise RuntimeError("generator didn't yield") from None
20 builtins.RuntimeError: generator didn't yield
```

Here we create an instance of our context manager and try running it twice with Python's with statement. The second time it runs, it raises a **RuntimeError**.

But what if we wanted to be able to run the context manager twice? Well we'd need to use one that is "reentrant". Let's use the **redirect_stdout** context manager that we used before!

>>> from contextlib import redirect_stdout >>> from io import StringIO >>> stream = StringIO() >>> write_to_stream = redirect_stdout(stream) >>> with write_to_stream: ... print('Write something to the stream') ... with write_to_stream: ... print('Write something else to stream') ... >>> print(stream.getvalue()) Write something to the stream Write something else to stream

Here we create a nested context manager where they both write to **StringIO**, which is an in-memory text stream. The reason this works instead of raising a RuntimeError like before is that redirect_-stdout is reentrant and allows us to call it twice. Of course, a real world example would be much more complex with more functions calling each other. Please also note that reentrant context managers are not necessarily thread-safe. Read the documentation before trying to use them in a thread.

Wrapping Up

Context managers are a lot of fun and come in handy all the time. I use them in my automated tests all the time for opening and closing dialogs, for example. Now you should be able to use some of Python's built-in tools to create your own context managers. Be sure to take the time to read the Python documentation on contextlib as there are lots of additional information that is not covered in this chapter. Have fun and happy coding!

Chapter 4 - The functools module

Python comes with a fun module called **functools**. The functions inside functools are considered "higher-order" functions which can act on or return other functions. In this chapter we will be looking at the following portions of the functools package:

- lru_cache
- partials
- singledispatch
- wraps

Let's get started by learning how to create a simple cache with Python!

Caching with functools.lru_cache

The functools module provides a handy decorator called **lru_cache**. Note that it was added in Python 3.2. According to the documentation, it will "wrap a function with a memoizing callable that saves up to the maxsize most recent calls". In other words, it's a decorator that adds caching to the function it decorates. Let's write a quick function based on the example from the functools documentation that will grab various web pages. In this case, we'll be grabbing pages from the Python documentation site.

```python
import urllib.error
import urllib.request

from functools import lru_cache


@lru_cache(maxsize=24)
def get_webpage(module):
    """
    Gets the specified Python module web page
    """
    webpage = "https://docs.python.org/3/library/{}.html".format(module)
```

```
13     try:
14         with urllib.request.urlopen(webpage) as request:
15             return request.read()
16         except urllib.error.HTTPError:
17         return None
18
19  if __name__ == '__main__':
20      modules = ['functools', 'collections', 'os', 'sys']
21      for module in modules:
22      page = get_webpage(module)
23      if page:
24          print("{} module page found".format(module))
```

In the code above, we decorate our **get_webpage** function with **lru_cache** and set its max size to 24 calls. Then we set up a webpage string variable and pass in which module we want our function to fetch. I found that this works best if you run it in a Python interpreter, such as IDLE. This alls you to run the loop a couple of times against the function. What you will quickly see is that the first time it runs the code, the output is printed our relatively slowly. But if you run it again in the same session, you will see that it prints immediately which demonstrates that the lru_cache has cached the calls correctly. Give this a try in your own interpreter instance to see the results for yourself.

There is also a **typed** parameter that we can pass to the decorator. It is a Boolean that tells the decorator to cache arguments of different types separately if typed is set to **True**.

functool.partial

One of the functools classes is the **partial** class. You can use it create a new function with partial application of the arguments and keywords that you pass to it. You can use partial to "freeze" a portion of your function's arguments and/or keywords which results in a new object. Another way to put it is that partial creates a new function with some defaults. Let's look at an example!

```
1  >>> from functools import partial
2  >>> def add(x, y):
3  ...        return x + y
4  ...
5  >>> p_add = partial(add, 2)
6  >>> p_add(4)
7  6
```

Here we create a simple adding function that returns the result of adding its arguments, x and y. Next we create a new callable by creating an instance of partial and passing it our function and an argument for that function. In other words, we are basically defaulting the x parameter of our add function to the number 2. Finally we call our new callable, p_add, with the argument of the number 4 which results in 6 because 2 + 4 = 6.

One handy use case for partials is to pass arguments to callbacks. Let's take a look using wxPython:

```python
import wx

from functools import partial


class MainFrame(wx.Frame):
    """
    This app shows a group of buttons
    """

    def __init__(self, *args, **kwargs):
        """Constructor"""
        super(MainFrame, self).__init__(parent=None, title='Partial')
        panel = wx.Panel(self)

        sizer = wx.BoxSizer(wx.VERTICAL)
        btn_labels = ['one', 'two', 'three']
        for label in btn_labels:
            btn = wx.Button(panel, label=label)
            btn.Bind(wx.EVT_BUTTON, partial(self.onButton, label=label))
            sizer.Add(btn, 0, wx.ALL, 5)

        panel.SetSizer(sizer)
        self.Show()

    def onButton(self, event, label):
        """
        Event handler called when a button is pressed
        """
        print('You pressed: ' + str(label))


if __name__ == '__main__':
    app = wx.App(False)
    frame = MainFrame()
    app.MainLoop()
```

Here we use partial to call the onButton event handler with an extra argument, which happens to be the button's label. This might not seem all that useful to you, but if you do much GUI programming, you'll see a lot of people asking how to do this sort of thing. Of course, you could also use a lambda instead for passing arguments to callbacks.

One use case that we've used at work was for our automated test framework. We test a UI with Python and we wanted to be able to pass a function along to dismiss certain dialogs. Basically you would pass a function along with the name of the dialog to dismiss, but it would need to be called at a certain point in the process to work correctly. Since I can't show that code, here's a really basic example of passing a partial function around:

```python
from functools import partial


def add(x, y):
    """"""
    return x + y


def multiply(x, y):
    """"""
    return x * y


def run(func):
    """"""
    print(func())


def main():
    """"""
    a1 = partial(add, 1, 2)
    m1 = partial(multiply, 5, 8)
    run(a1)
    run(m1)

if __name__ == "__main__":
    main()
```

Here we create a couple of partial functions in our main function. Next we pass those partials to our run function, call it and then print out the result of the function that was called.

Function Overloading with functools.singledispatch

Python fairly recently added partial support for function overloading in Python 3.4. They did this by adding a neat little decorator to the functools module called singledispatch. This decorator will transform your regular function into a single dispatch generic function. Note however that singledispatch only happens based on the first argument's type. Let's take a look at an example to see how this works!

```python
from functools import singledispatch


@singledispatch
def add(a, b):
    raise NotImplementedError('Unsupported type')


@add.register(int)
def _(a, b):
    print("First argument is of type ", type(a))
    print(a + b)


@add.register(str)
def _(a, b):
    print("First argument is of type ", type(a))
    print(a + b)


@add.register(list)
def _(a, b):
    print("First argument is of type ", type(a))
    print(a + b)


if __name__ == '__main__':
    add(1, 2)
    add('Python', 'Programming')
    add([1, 2, 3], [5, 6, 7])
```

Here we import singledispatch from functools and apply it to a simple function that we call add. This function is our catch-all function and will only get called if none of the other decorated functions handle the type passed. You will note that we currently handle integers, strings and lists as the first argument. If we were to call our add function with something else, such as a dictionary, then it would raise a NotImplementedError.

Try running the code yourself. You should see output that looks like this:

```
1   First argument is of type   <class 'int'>
2   3
3   First argument is of type   <class 'str'>
4   PythonProgramming
5   First argument is of type   <class 'list'>
6   [1, 2, 3, 5, 6, 7]
7   Traceback (most recent call last):
8     File "overloads.py", line 30, in <module>
9       add({}, 1)
10    File "/usr/local/lib/python3.5/functools.py", line 743, in wrapper
11      return dispatch(args[0].__class__)(*args, **kw)
12    File "overloads.py", line 5, in add
13      raise NotImplementedError('Unsupported type')
14  NotImplementedError: Unsupported type
```

As you can see, the code works exactly as advertised. It calls the appropriate function based on the first argument's type. If the type isn't handled, then we raise a NotImplementedError. If you want to know what types we are currently handling, you can add the following piece of code to the end of the file, preferable before the line that raises an error:

```
1   print(add.registry.keys())
```

This will print out something like this:

```
1   dict_keys([<class 'str'>, <class 'int'>, <class 'list'>, <class 'object'>])
```

This tells us that we can handle strings, integers, lists and objects (the default). The singledispatch decorator also supports decorator stacking. This allows us to create an overloaded function that can handle multiple types. Let's take a look:

```
1  from functools import singledispatch
2  from decimal import Decimal
3
4
5  @singledispatch
6  def add(a, b):
7      raise NotImplementedError('Unsupported type')
8
9
10 @add.register(float)
11 @add.register(Decimal)
12 def _(a, b):
13     print("First argument is of type ", type(a))
14     print(a + b)
15
16
17 if __name__ == '__main__':
18     add(1.23, 5.5)
19     add(Decimal(100.5), Decimal(10.789))
```

This basically tells Python that one of the add function overloads can handle float and decimal.Decimal types as the first argument. If you run this code, you should see something like the following:

```
1  First argument is of type  <class 'float'>
2  6.73
3  First argument is of type  <class 'decimal.Decimal'>
4  111.2889999999999997015720510
5  dict_keys([<class 'float'>, <class 'int'>, <class 'object'>, <class 'decimal.Dec\
6  imal'>
```

You may have noticed this already, but because of the way all these functions were written, you could stack the decorators to handle all the cases in the previous example and this example into one overloaded function. However, in a normal overloaded case, each overload would call different code instead of doing the same thing.

functools.wraps

There is a little known tool that I wanted to cover in this section. It is called **wraps** and it too is a part of the functools module. You can use wraps as a decorator to fix docstrings and names of decorated functions. Why does this matter? This sounds like a weird edge case at first, but if you're writing an API or any code that someone other than yourself will be using, then this could be important. The reason being that when you use Python's introspection to figure out someone else's code, a decorated function will return the wrong information. Let's look at a simple example that I have dubbed decorum.py:

```python
1   # decorum.py
2
3
4   def another_function(func):
5       """
6       A function that accepts another function
7       """
8
9       def wrapper():
10          """
11          A wrapping function
12          """
13          val = "The result of %s is %s" % (func(),
14                                             eval(func())
15                                             )
16          return val
17      return wrapper
18
19
20  @another_function
21  def a_function():
22      """A pretty useless function"""
23      return "1+1"
24
25
26  if __name__ == "__main__":
27      print(a_function.__name__)
28      print(a_function.__doc__)
```

In this code, we decorate the function called a_function with another_function. You can check a_-function's name and docstring by printing them out using the function's __name__ and __doc__-properties. If you run this example, you'll get the following for output:

```
1   wrapper
2
3   A wrapping function
```

That's not right! If you run this program in IDLE or the interpreter, it becomes even more obvious how this can get really confusing, really quickly.

```
1   >>> import decorum
2   >>> help(decorum)
3   Help on module decorum:
4
5   NAME
6       decorum -
7
8   FILE
9       /home/mike/decorum.py
10
11  FUNCTIONS
12      a_function = wrapper()
13          A wrapping function
14
15      another_function(func)
16          A function that accepts another function
17
18  >>> help(decorum.a_function)
19  Help on function other_func in module decorum:
20
21  wrapper()
22      A wrapping function
```

Basically what is happening here is that the decorator is changing the decorated function's name and docstring to its own.

Wraps to the Rescue!

How do we fix this little mess? The Python developers have given us the solution in functools.wraps! Let's check it out:

```python
1   from functools import wraps
2
3
4   def another_function(func):
5       """
6       A function that accepts another function
7       """
8
9       @wraps(func)
10      def wrapper():
```

```
11              """
12              A wrapping function
13              """
14              val = "The result of %s is %s" % (func(),
15                                                 eval(func())
16                                                )
17              return val
18      return wrapper
19
20
21  @another_function
22  def a_function():
23      """A pretty useless function"""
24      return "1+1"
25
26
27  if __name__ == "__main__":
28      #a_function()
29      print(a_function.__name__)
30      print(a_function.__doc__)
```

Here we import wraps from the functools module and use it as a decorator for the nested wrapper function inside of another_function. If you run it this time, the output will have changed:

```
1  a_function
2  A pretty useless function
```

Now we have the right name and docstring once more. If you go into your Python interpreter, the help function will now work correctly as well. I'll skip putting its output here and leave that for you to try.

Wrapping Up

Let's review. In this chapter, you learned some basic caching using **lru_cache**. Then we moved onto **partials** which lets you "freeze" a portion of your function's arguments and/or keywords allowing you to create a new object that you can call. Next we used **singledispatch** to overload functions with Python. While it only allows function overloading based on the first argument, this is still a handy tool to add to your arsenal! Finally we looked at **wraps** which had a very narrow focus: namely it fixes docstrings and function names that have been decorated such that they don't have the decorator's docstring or name any more.

Chapter 5 - All About Imports

One of the first items you learn as a beginner Python programmer is how to import other modules or packages. However, I've noticed that even people who have used Python casually for multiple years don't always know how flexible Python's importing infrastructure is. In this article, we will be looking at the following topics:

- Regular imports
- Using from
- Relative imports
- Optional imports
- Local imports
- import Pitfalls

Let's start off by looking at regular imports!

Regular Imports

A regular import, and quite possibly the most popular goes like this:

```
1  import sys
```

All you need to do is use the word "import" and then specify what module or package you want to actually import. The nice thing about import though is that it can also import multiple package at once:

```
1  import os, sys, time
```

While this is a space-saver, it's goes against the Python Style Guide's recommendations of putting each import on its own line.

Sometimes when you import a module, you want to rename it. Python supports this quite easily:

```
1  import sys as system
2
3  print(system.platform)
```

This piece of code simply renames our import to "system". We can call all of the modules methods the same way before, but with the new name. There are also certain submodules that have to be imported using dot notation:

```
1  import urllib.error
```

You won't see these very often, but they're good to know about.

Using "from module import something"

There are many times when you just want to import part of a module or library. Let's see how Python accomplishes this:

```
1  from functools import lru_cache
```

What the code above does is allow you to call lru_cache directly. If you had imported just functools the normal way, then you would have to call lru_cache using something like this:

```
1  functools.lru_cache(*args)
```

Depending on what you're doing, the above might actually be a good thing. In complex code bases, it's quite nice to know where something has been imported from. However, if your code is well maintained and modularized properly, importing just a portion from the module can be quite handy and more succinct.

Of course you can also use the from method to import everything, like so:

```
1  from os import *
```

This is handy in rare circumstances, but it can also really mess up your namespace. The problem is that you might define your own function or a top level variable that has the same name as one of the items you imported and if you try to use the one from the os module, it will use yours instead. So you end up with a rather confusing logic error. The Tkinter module is really the only one in the standard library that I've seen recommended to be imported in total.

If you happen to write your own module or package, some people recommend importing everything in your __init__.py to make your module or package easier to use. Personally I prefer explicit to implicit, but to each their own.

You can also meet somewhere in the middle by importing multiple items from a package:

```
1  from os import path, walk, unlink
2  from os import uname, remove
```

In the code above, we import five functions from the os module. You will also note that we can do so by importing from the same module multiple times. If you would rather, you can also use parentheses to import lots of items:

```
1  from os import (path, walk, unlink, uname,
2              remove, rename)
```

This is useful technique, but you can do it another way too:

```
1  from os import path, walk, unlink, uname, \
2              remove, rename
```

The backslash you see above is Python's line continuation character, which tells Python that this line of code continues on the following line.

Relative Imports

PEP 328 describes how relative imports came about and what specific syntax was chosen. The idea behind it was to use periods to determine how to relatively import other packages / modules. The reason was to prevent the accidental shadowing of standard library modules. Let's use the example folder structure that PEP 328 suggests and see if we can get it to work:

```
1  my_package/
2      __init__.py
3      subpackage1/
4          __init__.py
5          module_x.py
6          module_y.py
7      subpackage2/
8          __init__.py
9          module_z.py
10     module_a.py
```

Create the files and folders above somewhere on your hard drive. In the top-level __init__.py, put the following code in place:

```
1   from . import subpackage1
2   from . import subpackage2
```

Next navigate down in subpackage1 and edit its __init__.py to have the following contents:

```
1   from . import module_x
2   from . import module_y
```

Now edit module_x.py such that is has the following code:

```
1   from .module_y import spam as ham
2
3   def main():
4       ham()
```

Finally edit module_y.py to match this:

```
1   def spam():
2       print('spam ' * 3)
```

Open a terminal and cd to the folder that has my_package, but not into my_package. Run the Python interpreter in this folder. I'm using iPython below mainly because its auto-completion is so handy:

```
1   In [1]: import my_package
2
3   In [2]: my_package.subpackage1.module_x
4   Out[2]: <module 'my_package.subpackage1.module_x' from 'my_package/subpackage1/m\
5   odule_x.py'>
6
7   In [3]: my_package.subpackage1.module_x.main()
8   spam spam spam
```

Relative imports are great for creating code that you turn into packages. If you have created a lot of code that is related, then this is probably the way to go. You will find that relative imports are used in many popular packages on the Python Packages Index (PyPI). Also note that if you need to go more than one level, you can just use additional periods. However, according to PEP 328, you really shouldn't go above two.

Also note that if you were to add an "if __name__ == â€˜__main__'" portion to the module_x.py and tried to run it, you would end up with a rather confusing error. Let's edit the file and give it a try!

```
1  from . module_y import spam as ham
2
3  def main():
4      ham()
5
6  if __name__ == '__main__':
7      # This won't work!
8      main()
```

Now navigate into the subpackage1 folder in your terminal and run the following command:

```
1  python module_x.py
```

You should see the following error on your screen for Python 2:

```
1  Traceback (most recent call last):
2    File "module_x.py", line 1, in <module>
3      from . module_y import spam as ham
4  ValueError: Attempted relative import in non-package
```

And if you tried to run it with Python 3, you'd get this:

```
1  Traceback (most recent call last):
2    File "module_x.py", line 1, in <module>
3      from . module_y import spam as ham
4  SystemError: Parent module '' not loaded, cannot perform relative import
```

What this means is that module_x.py is a module inside of a package and you're trying to run it as a script, which is incompatible with relative imports.

If you'd like to use this module in your code, you will have to add it to Python's import search path. The easiest way to do that is as follows:

```
1  import sys
2  sys.path.append('/path/to/folder/containing/my_package')
3  import my_package
```

Note that you want the path to the folder right above my_package, not my_package itself. The reason is that my_package is THE package, so if you append that, you'll have issues using the package. Let's move on to optional imports!

Optional Imports

Optional imports are used when you have a preferred module or package that you want to use, but you also want a fallback in case it doesn't exist. You might use optional imports to support multiple versions of software or for speed ups, for example. Here's an example from the package github2 that demonstrates how you might use optional imports to support different versions of Python:

```python
try:
    # For Python 3
    from http.client import responses
except ImportError:  # For Python 2.5-2.7
    try:
        from httplib import responses  # NOQA
    except ImportError:  # For Python 2.4
        from BaseHTTPServer import BaseHTTPRequestHandler as _BHRH
        responses = dict([(k, v[0]) for k, v in _BHRH.responses.items()])
```

The lxml package also makes use of optional imports:

```python
try:
    from urlparse import urljoin
    from urllib2 import urlopen
except ImportError:
    # Python 3
    from urllib.parse import urljoin
    from urllib.request import urlopen
```

As you can see, it's used all the time to great effect and is a handy tool to add to your repertoire.

Local Imports

A local import is when you import a module into local scope. When you do your imports at the top of your Python script file, that is importing the module into your global scope, which means that any functions or methods that follow will be able to use it. Let's look at how importing into a local scope works:

```
1   import sys  # global scope
2
3   def square_root(a):
4       # This import is into the square_root functions local scope
5       import math
6       return math.sqrt(a)
7
8   def my_pow(base_num, power):
9       return math.pow(base_num, power)
10
11  if __name__ == '__main__':
12      print(square_root(49))
13      print(my_pow(2, 3))
```

Here we import the sys module into the global scope, but we don't actually use it. Then in the square_root function we import Python's math module into the function's local scope, which means that the math module can only be used inside of the square_root function. IF we try to use it in the my_pow function, we will receive a NameError. Go ahead and try running the code to see this in action!

One of the benefits of using local scope is that you might be using a module that takes a long time to load. If so, it might make sense to put it into a function that is called rarely rather than your module's global scope. It really depends on what you want to do. Frankly, I've almost never used imports into the local scope, mostly because it can be hard to tell what's going on if the imports are scattered all over the module. Conventionally, all imports should be at the top of the module after all.

Import Pitfalls

There are some very common import pitfalls that programmers fall into. We'll go over the two most common here:

- Circular imports
- Shadowed imports

Let's start by looking at circular imports

Circular Imports

Circular imports happen when you create two modules that import each other. Let's look at an example as that will make it quite clear what I'm referring to. Put the following code into a module called a.py

```
1  # a.py
2  import b
3
4  def a_test():
5      print("in a_test")
6      b.b_test()
7
8  a_test()
```

Then create another module in the same folder as the one above and name it b.py

```
1  # b.py
2  import a
3
4  def b_test():
5      print('In test_b"')
6      a.a_test()
7
8  b_test()
```

If you run either of these modules, you should receive an AttributeError. This happens because both modules are attempting to import each other. Basically what's happening here is that module a is trying to import module b, but it can't do that because module b is attempting to import module a which is already being executed. I've read about some hacky workarounds but in general you should just refactor your code to prevent this kind of thing from happening

Shadowed Imports

Shadow imports (AKA name masking) happen when the programmer creates a module with the same name as a Python module. Let's create a contrived example! In this case, create a file named math.py and put the following code inside it:

```
1  import math
2
3  def square_root(number):
4      return math.sqrt(number)
5
6  square_root(72)
```

Now open a terminal and try running this code. When I tried this, I got the following traceback:

```
1  Traceback (most recent call last):
2    File "math.py", line 1, in <module>
3      import math
4    File "/Users/michael/Desktop/math.py", line 6, in <module>
5      square_root(72)
6    File "/Users/michael/Desktop/math.py", line 4, in square_root
7      return math.sqrt(number)
8  AttributeError: module 'math' has no attribute 'sqrt'
```

What happened here? Well when you run this code, the first place Python looks for a module called "math" is in the currently running script's folder. In this case, it finds the module we're running and tries to use that. But our module doesn't have a function or attribute called sqrt, so an AttributeError is raised.

Wrapping Up

We've covered a lot of ground in this article and there's still a lot more to learn about Python's importing system. There's PEP 302 which covers import hooks and allows you to do some really cool things, like import directly from github. There's also Python's importlib which is well worth taking a look at. Get out there and start digging in the source code to learn about even more neat tricks. Happy coding!

Chapter 6 - The importlib Module

Python provides the **importlib** package as part of its standard library of modules. Its purpose is to provide the implementation to Python's **import** statement (and the __import__() function). In addition, importlib gives the programmer the ability to create their own custom objects (AKA an **importer**) that can be used in the import process.

What about imp?

There is another module called **imp** that provides an interface to the mechanisms behind Python's **import** statement. This module was deprecated in Python 3.4. It is intended that **importlib** should be used in its place.

This module is pretty complicated, so we'll be limiting the scope of this chapter to the following topics:

- Dynamic imports
- Checking is a module can be imported
- Importing from the source file itself
- A clever 3rd party module called import_from_github_com

Let's get started by looking at dynamic imports!

Dynamic Imports

The importlib module supports the ability to import a module that is passed to it as a string. So let's create a couple of simple modules that we can work with. We will give both modules the same interface, but have them print their names so we can tell the difference between the two. Create two modules with different names such as **foo.py** and **bar.py** and add the following code in each of them:

```
1  def main():
2      print(__name__)
```

Now we just need to use importlib to import them. Let's look at some code to do just that. Make sure that you put this code in the same folder as the two modules you created above.

```
1   # importer.py}
2   import importlib
3
4
5   def dynamic_import(module):
6
7       return importlib.import_module(module)
8
9
10  if __name__ == '__main__':
11      module = dynamic_import('foo')
12      module.main()
13
14      module_two = dynamic_import('bar')
15      module_two.main()
```

Here we import the handy importlib module and create a really simple function called **dynamic_-import**. All this function does is call importlib's **import_module** function with the module string that we passed in and returns the result of that call. Then in our conditional statement at the bottom, we call each module's **main** method, which will dutifully print out the name of the module.

You probably won't be doing this a lot in your own code, but occasionally you'll find yourself wanting to import a module when you only have the module as a string. The importlib module gives us the ability to do just that.

Module Import Checking

Python has a coding style that is known as EAFP: Easier to ask for forgiveness than permission. What this means is that it's often easier to just assume that something exists (like a key in a dict) and catch an exception if we're wrong. You saw this in our previous chapter where we would attempt to import a module and we caught the **ImportError** if it didn't exist. What if we wanted to check and see if a module could be imported rather than just guessing? You can do that with importlib! Let's take a look:

```
1   import importlib.util
2
3   def check_module(module_name):
4       """
5       Checks if module can be imported without actually
6       importing it
7       """
8       module_spec = importlib.util.find_spec(module_name)
9       if module_spec is None:
10          print('Module: {} not found'.format(module_name))
11          return None
12      else:
13          print('Module: {} can be imported!'.format(module_name))
14          return module_spec
15
16
17  def import_module_from_spec(module_spec):
18      """
19      Import the module via the passed in module specification
20      Returns the newly imported module
21      """
22      module = importlib.util.module_from_spec(module_spec)
23      module_spec.loader.exec_module(module)
24      return module
25
26  if __name__ == '__main__':
27      module_spec = check_module('fake_module')
28      module_spec = check_module('collections')
29      if module_spec:
30          module = import_module_from_spec(module_spec)
31          print(dir(module))
```

Here we import a submodule of importlib called **util**. The **check_module** code has the first piece of magic that we want to look at. In it we call the **find_spec** function against the module string that we passed in. First we pass in a fake name and then we pass in a real name of a Python module. If you run this code, you will see that when you pass in a module name that is not installed, the **find_spec** function will return **None** and our code will print out that the module was not found. If it was found, then we will return the module specification.

We can take that module specification and use it to actually import the module. Or you could just pass the string to the **import_module** function that we learned about in the previous section. But we already covered that so let's learn how to use the module specification. Take a look at the **import_-module_from_spec** function in the code above. It accepts the module specification that was returned by **check_module**. We then pass that into importlib's **module_from_spec** function, which returns the import module. Python's documentation recommends executing the module after importing it, so that's what we do next with the **exec_module** function. Finally we return the module and run Python's **dir** against it to make sure it's the module we expect.

Import From Source File

The importlib's util sub-module has another neat trick that I want to cover. You can use **util** to import a module using just it's name and file path. The following is a very derived example, but I think it will get the point across:

```
1   import importlib.util
2
3   def import_source(module_name):
4       module_file_path = module_name.__file__
5       module_name = module_name.__name__
6
7       module_spec = importlib.util.spec_from_file_location(
8           module_name, module_file_path)
9       module = importlib.util.module_from_spec(module_spec)
10      module_spec.loader.exec_module(module)
11      print(dir(module))
12
13      msg = 'The {module_name} module has the following methods:' \
14          ' {methods}'
15      print(msg.format(module_name=module_name,
16                       methods=dir(module)))
17
18  if __name__ == '__main__':
19      import logging
20      import_source(logging)
```

In the code above, we actually import the **logging** module and pass it to our **import_source** function. Once there, we grab the module's actual path and its name. Then we call pass those pieces of information into the util's **spec_from_file_location** function which will return the module's specification. Once we have that, we can use the same importlib mechanisms that we used in the previous section to actually import the module.

Now let's look at a neat 3rd party module that Python's **__import__()** function to import packages directly from github!

import_from_github_com

There's a neat package called **import_from_github_com** that can be used to find and load modules from github. To install it, all you need to do is use **pip** like this:

```
1  pip install import_from_github_com
```

The package uses the new import hooks provided in PEP 302 to basically allow you to import a package from github. What the package actually appears to do is install the package and add it to **locals**. Regardless, you will need Python 3.2 or greater, **git** and **pip** to use this package.

Once those are installed, you can try doing this in your Python shell:

```
1   >>> from github_com.zzzeek import sqlalchemy
2   Collecting git+https://github.com/zzzeek/sqlalchemy
3     Cloning https://github.com/zzzeek/sqlalchemy to /tmp/pip-acfv7t06-build
4   Installing collected packages: SQLAlchemy
5     Running setup.py install for SQLAlchemy ... done
6   Successfully installed SQLAlchemy-1.1.0b1.dev0
7   >>> locals()
8   {'__builtins__': <module 'builtins' (built-in)>, '__spec__': None,
9    '__package__': None, '__doc__': None, '__name__': '__main__',
10  'sqlalchemy': <module 'sqlalchemy' from '/usr/local/lib/python3.5/site-packages/\
11  sqlalchemy/__init__.py'>,
12   '__loader__': <class '_frozen_importlib.BuiltinImporter'>}
```

If you take a look at the source code for import_from_github_com, you will notice that it isn't using **importlib**. Instead it uses pip to install the package if it's not installed and then it uses Python's **__import__()** function to actually import the newly installed module. It's a really clever piece of code that is well worth studying.

Wrapping Up

At this point, you should have an idea of how you might use importlib and import hooks in your own code. There is a lot more to this module than what is covered in this chapter, so if you have a need to write a custom importer or loader then you'll want to spend some time reading the documentation and the source code.

Chapter 7 - Iterators and Generators

You have probably been using iterators and generators since you started programming in Python but you may not have realized it. In this chapter, we will learn what an iterator and a generator are. We will also be learning how they are created so we can create our own should we need to.

Iterators

An iterator is an object that will allow you to iterate over a container. The iterator in Python is implemented via two distinct methods: **__iter__** and **__next__**. The **__iter__** method is required for your container to provide iteration support. It will return the iterator object itself. But if you want to create an iterator object, then you will need to define **__next__** as well, which will return the next item in the container.

Note: In Python 2, the naming convention was slightly different. You still needed __iter__, but __next__ was called **next.***

To make things extra clear, let's go over a couple of definitions:

- iterable - an object that has the __iter__ method defined
- iterator - an object that has both __iter__ and __next__ defined where __iter__ will return the iterator object and __next__ will return the next element in the iteration.

As with most magic methods (the methods with double-underscores), you should not call __iter__ or __next__ directly. Instead you can use a **for** loop or list comprehension and Python will call the methods for you automatically. There are cases when you may need to call them, but you can do so with Python's built-ins: **iter** and **next**.

Before we move on, I want to mention Sequences. Python 3 has several sequence types such as list, tuple and range. The list is an iterable, but not an iterator because it does not implement __next__. This can be easily seen in the following example:

```
1  >>> my_list = [1, 2, 3]
2  >>> next(my_list)
3  Traceback (most recent call last):
4    Python Shell, prompt 2, line 1
5  builtins.TypeError: 'list' object is not an iterator
```

When we tried to call the list's next method in the example above, we received a **TypeError** and were informed that the list object is not an iterator. But we can make it one! Let's see how:

```
1  >>> iter(my_list)
2  <list_iterator object at 0x7faaaa477a58>
3  >>> list_iterator = iter(my_list)
4  >>> next(list_iterator)
5  1
6  >>> next(list_iterator)
7  2
8  >>> next(list_iterator)
9  3
10 >>> next(list_iterator)
11 Traceback (most recent call last):
12   Python Shell, prompt 8, line 1
13 builtins.StopIteration:
```

To turn the list into an iterator, just wrap it in a call to Python's **iter** method. Then you can call **next** on it until the iterator runs out of items and **StopIteration** gets raised. Let's try turning the list into an iterator and iterating over it with a loop:

```
1  >>> for item in iter(my_list):
2  ...      print(item)
3  ...
4  1
5  2
6  3
```

When you use a loop to iterate over the iterator, you don't need to call next and you also don't have to worry about the StopIteration exception being raised.

Creating Your Own Iterators

Occasionally you will want to create your own custom iterators. Python makes this very easy to do. As mentioned in the previous section, all you need to do is implement the __iter__ and __next__-methods in your class. Let's create an iterator that can iterate over a string of letters:

```
 1   class MyIterator:
 2
 3       def __init__(self, letters):
 4           """
 5           Constructor
 6           """
 7           self.letters = letters
 8           self.position = 0
 9
10       def __iter__(self):
11           """
12           Returns itself as an iterator
13           """
14           return self
15
16       def __next__(self):
17           """
18           Returns the next letter in the sequence or
19           raises StopIteration
20           """
21           if self.position >= len(self.letters):
22               raise StopIteration
23           letter = self.letters[self.position]
24           self.position += 1
25           return letter
26
27   if __name__ == '__main__':
28       i = MyIterator('abcd')
29       for item in i:
30           print(item)
```

For this example, we only needed three methods in our class. In our initialization, we pass in the string of letters and create a class variable to refer to them. We also initialize a position variable so we always know where we're at in the string. The __iter__ method just returns itself, which is all it really needs to do. The __next__ method is the meatiest part of this class. Here we check the position against the length of the string and raise StopIteration if we try to go past its length. Otherwise we extract the letter we're on, increment the position and return the letter.

Let's take a moment to create an infinite iterator. An infinite iterator is one that can iterate forever. You will need to be careful when calling these as they will cause an infinite loop if you don't make sure to put a bound on them.

```
1   class Doubler:
2       """
3       An infinite iterator
4       """
5
6       def __init__(self):
7           """
8           Constructor
9           """
10          self.number = 0
11
12      def __iter__(self):
13          """
14          Returns itself as an iterator
15          """
16          return self
17
18      def __next__(self):
19          """
20          Doubles the number each time next is called
21          and returns it.
22          """
23          self.number += 1
24          return self.number * self.number
25
26  if __name__ == '__main__':
27      doubler = Doubler()
28      count = 0
29
30      for number in doubler:
31          print(number)
32          if count > 5:
33              break
34          count += 1
```

In this piece of code, we don't pass anything to our iterator. We just instantiate it. Then to make sure we don't end up in an infinite loop, we add a counter before we start iterating over our custom iterator. Finally we start iterating and break out when the counter goes above 5.

Generators

A normal Python function will always return one value, whether it be a list, an integer or some other object. But what if you wanted to be able to call a function and have it yield a series of values? That is where generators come in. A generator works by "saving" where it last left off (or yielding) and giving the calling function a value. So instead of returning the execution to the caller, it just gives temporary control back. To do this magic, a generator function requires Python's **yield** statement.

Side-note: In other languages, a generator might be called a coroutine.*

Let's take a moment and create a simple generator!

```
1  >>> def doubler_generator():
2  ...     number = 2
3  ...     while True:
4  ...         yield number
5  ...         number *= number
6  >>> doubler = doubler_generator()
7  >>> next(doubler)
8  2
9  >>> next(doubler)
10 4
11 >>> next(doubler)
12 16
13 >>> type(doubler)
14 <class 'generator'>
```

This particular generator will basically create an infinite sequence. You can call **next** on it all day long and it will never run out of values to yield. Because you can iterate over a generator, a generator is considered to be a type of iterator, but no one really refers to them as such. But underneath the covers, the generator is also defining the **__next__** method that we looked at in our previous section, which is why the **next** keyword we just used worked.

Let's look at another example that only yields 3 items instead of an infinite sequence!

```
1   >>> def silly_generator():
2   ...     yield "Python"
3   ...     yield "Rocks"
4   ...     yield "So do you!"
5   >>> gen = silly_generator()
6   >>> next(gen)
7   'Python'
8   >>> next(gen)
9   'Rocks'
10  >>> next(gen)
11  'So do you!'
12  >>> next(gen)
13  Traceback (most recent call last):
14    Python Shell, prompt 21, line 1
15  builtins.StopIteration:
```

Here we have a generator that uses the **yield** statement 3 times. In each instance, it yields a different string. You can think of **yield** as the **return** statement for a generator. Whenever you call yield, the function stops and saves its state. Then it yields the value out, which is why you see something getting printed out to the terminal in the example above. If we'd had variables in our function, those variables would be saved too.

When you see **StopIteration**, you know that you have exhausted the iterator. This means that it ran out of items. This is normal behavior in all iterators as you saw the same thing happen in the iterators section.

Anyway when we call **next** again, the generator begins where it left off and yields whatever the next value is or we finish the function and the generator stops. On the other hand, if you never call next again, then the state will eventually go away.

Let's reinstantiate the generator and try looping over it!

```
1   >>> gen = silly_generator()
2   >>> for item in gen:
3   ...     print(item)
4   ...
5   Python
6   Rocks
7   So do you!
```

The reason we create a new instance of the generator is that if we tried looping over it, nothing would be yielded. This is because we already ran through all the values in that particular instance of the generator. So in this example, we create the new instance, loop over it and print out the values that are yielded. The **for** loop once again handles the **StopIteration** exception for us and just breaks out of the loop when the generator is exhausted.

One of the biggest benefits to a generator is that it can iterate over large data sets and return them one piece at a time. This is what happens when we open a file and return it line-by-line:

```
1  with open('/path/to/file.txt') as fobj:
2      for line in fobj:
3          # process the line
```

Python basically turns the file object into a generator when we iterate over it in this manner. This allows us to process files that are too large to load into memory. You will find generators useful for any large data set that you need to work with in chunks or when you need to generate a large data set that would otherwise fill up your all your computer's memory.

Wrapping Up

At this point you should now understand what an iterator is and how to use one. You should also know the difference between an iterable and an iterator. Finally, we learned what a generator is and why you might want to use one. For example, a generator is great for memory efficient data processing. In the next chapter, we will dig into an iterator library that is included with Python that's called **itertools**.

Chapter 8 - The itertools Module

Python provides a great module for creating your own iterators. The module I am referring to is **itertools**. The tools provided by itertools are fast and memory efficient. You will be able to take these building blocks to create your own specialized iterators that can be used for efficient looping. In this chapter, we will be looking at examples of each building block so that by the end you will understand how to use them for your own code bases.

Let's get started by looking at some infinite iterators!

The Infinite Iterators

The itertools package comes with three iterators that can iterate infinitely. What this means is that when you use them, you need to understand that you will need to break out of these iterators eventually or you'll have an infinite loop.

These can be useful for generating numbers or cycling over iterables of unknown length, for example. Let's get started learning about these interesting iterables!

count(start=0, step=1)

The **count** iterator will return evenly spaced values starting with the number you pass in as its **start** parameter. Count also accept a **step** parameter. Let's take a look at a simple example:

```
1  >>> from itertools import count
2  >>> for i in count(10):
3  ...     if i > 20:
4  ...         break
5  ...     else:
6  ...         print(i)
7  ...
8  10
9  11
10 12
11 13
```

```
12  14
13  15
14  16
15  17
16  18
17  19
18  20
```

Here we import **count** from itertools and we create a **for** loop. We add a conditional check that will break out of the loop should the iterator exceed 20, otherwise it prints out where we are in the iterator. You will note that the output starts at 10 as that was what we passed to **count** as our start value.

Another way to limit the output of this infinite iterator is to use another sub-module from itertools, namely **islice**. Here's how:

```
1  >>> from itertools import islice
2  >>> for i in islice(count(10), 5):
3  ...     print(i)
4  ...
5  10
6  11
7  12
8  13
9  14
```

In this example we import **islice** and we loop over **count** starting at 10 and ending after 5 items. As you may have guessed, the second argument to islice is when to stop iterating. But it doesn't mean "stop when I reach the number 5". Instead, it means "stop when we've reached five iterations".

cycle(iterable)

The **cycle** iterator from itertools allows you to create an iterator that will cycle through a series of values infinitely. Let's pass it a 3 letter string and see what happens:

```
1  >>> from itertools import cycle
2  >>> count = 0
3  >>> for item in cycle('XYZ'):
4  ...     if count > 7:
5  ...         break
6  ...     print(item)
7  ...     count += 1
8  ...
9  X
10 Y
11 Z
12 X
13 Y
14 Z
15 X
16 Y
```

Here we create a **for** loop to loop over the infinite cycle of the three letter: XYZ. Of course, we don't want to actually cycle forever, so we add a simple counter to break out of the loop with.

You can also use Python's **next** built-in to iterate over the iterators you create with itertools:

```
1  >>> polys = ['triangle', 'square', 'pentagon', 'rectangle']
2  >>> iterator = cycle(polys)
3  >>> next(iterator)
4  'triangle'
5  >>> next(iterator)
6  'square'
7  >>> next(iterator)
8  'pentagon'
9  >>> next(iterator)
10 'rectangle'
11 >>> next(iterator)
12 'triangle'
13 >>> next(iterator)
14 'square'
```

In the code above, we create a simple list of polygons and pass them to **cycle**. We save our new iterator to a variable and then we pass that variable to the **next** function. Every time we call next, it returns the next value in the iterator. Since this iterator is infinite, we can call next all day long and never run out of items.

repeat(object)

The **repeat** iterators will return an object an object over and over again forever unless you set its **times** argument. It is quite similar to **cycle** except that it doesn't cycle over a set of values repeatedly. Let's take a look at a simple example:

```
1   >>> from itertools import repeat
2   >>> repeat(5, 5)
3   repeat(5, 5)
4   >>> iterator = repeat(5, 5)
5   >>> next(iterator)
6   5
7   >>> next(iterator)
8   5
9   >>> next(iterator)
10  5
11  >>> next(iterator)
12  5
13  >>> next(iterator)
14  5
15  >>> next(iterator)
16  Traceback (most recent call last):
17    Python Shell, prompt 21, line 1
18  builtins.StopIteration:
```

Here we import **repeat** and tell it to repeat the number 5 five times. Then we call **next** on our new iterator six times to see if it works correctly. When you run this code, you will see that **StopIteration** gets raised because we have run out of values in our iterator.

Iterators That Terminate

Most of the iterators that you create with itertools are not infinite. In this sections, we will be studying the finite iterators of itertools. To get output that is readable, we will be using Python's built-in **list** type. If you do not use **list**, then you will only get an itertools object printed out.

accumulate(iterable)

The **accumulate** iterator will return accumulated sums or the accumulated results of a two argument function that you can pass to **accumulate**. The default of accumulate is addition, so let's give that a quick try:

```
1  >>> from itertools import accumulate
2  >>> list(accumulate(range(10)))
3  [0, 1, 3, 6, 10, 15, 21, 28, 36, 45]
```

Here we import **accumulate** and pass it a range of 10 numbers, 0-9. It adds each of them in turn, so the first is 0, the second is 0+1, the 3rd is 1+2, etc. Now let's import the **operator** module and add it into the mix:

```
1  >>> import operator
2  >>> list(accumulate(range(1, 5), operator.mul))
3  [1, 2, 6, 24]
```

Here we pass the number 1-4 to our **accumulate** iterator. We also pass it a function: **operator.mul**. This functions accepts to arguments to be multiplied. So for each iteration, it multiplies instead of adds (1x1=1, 1x2=2, 2x3=6, etc).

The documentation for accumulate shows some other interesting examples such as the amortization of a loan or the chaotic recurrence relation. You should definitely give those examples a look as they are will worth your time.

chain(*iterables)

The **chain** iterator will take a series of iterables and basically flatten them down into one long iterable. I actually recently needed its assistance in a project I was helping with. Basically we had a list with some items already in it and two other lists that we wanted to add to the original list, but we only wanted to append the items in each list to the original list instead of creating a list of lists. Originally I tried something like this:

```
1  >>> my_list = ['foo', 'bar']
2  >>> numbers = list(range(5))
3  >>> cmd = ['ls', '/some/dir']
4  >>> my_list.extend(cmd, numbers)
5  >>> my_list
6  ['foo', 'bar', ['ls', '/some/dir'], [0, 1, 2, 3, 4]]
```

Well that didn't work quite the way I wanted it to. The itertools module provides a much more elegant way of flattening these lists into one using **chain**:

```
1  >>> from itertools import chain
2  >>> my_list = list(chain(['foo', 'bar'], cmd, numbers))
3  >>> my_list
4  ['foo', 'bar', 'ls', '/some/dir', 0, 1, 2, 3, 4]
```

My more astute readers might notice that there's actually another way we could have accomplished the same thing without using itertools. You could do this to get the same effect:

```
1  >>> my_list = ['foo', 'bar']
2  >>> my_list += cmd + numbers
3  >>> my_list
4  ['foo', 'bar', 'ls', '/some/dir', 0, 1, 2, 3, 4]
```

Both of these methods are certainly valid and before I knew about **chain** I would have probably gone this route, but I think chain is a more elegant and easier to understand solution in this particular case.

chain.from_iterable(iterable)

You can also use a method of **chain** called **from_iterable**. This method works slightly differently then using chain directly. Instead of passing in a series of iterables, you have to pass in a nested list. Let's take a look:

```
1  >>> from itertools import chain
2  >>> numbers = list(range(5))
3  >>> cmd = ['ls', '/some/dir']
4  >>> chain.from_iterable(cmd, numbers)
5  Traceback (most recent call last):
6    Python Shell, prompt 66, line 1
7  builtins.TypeError: from_iterable() takes exactly one argument (2 given)
8  >>> list(chain.from_iterable([cmd, numbers]))
9  ['ls', '/some/dir', 0, 1, 2, 3, 4]
```

Here we import chain as we did previously. We try passing in our two lists but we end up getting a **TypeError**! To fix this, we change our call slightly such that we put **cmd** and **numbers** inside a **list** and then pass that nested list to **from_iterable**. It's a subtle difference but still easy to use!

compress(data, selectors)

The **compress** sub-module is useful for filtering the first iterable with the second. This works by making the second iterable a list of Booleans (or ones and zeroes which amounts to the same thing). Here's how it works:

```
1  >>> from itertools import compress
2  >>> letters = 'ABCDEFG'
3  >>> bools = [True, False, True, True, False]
4  >>> list(compress(letters, bools))
5  ['A', 'C', 'D']
```

In this example, we have a group of seven letters and a list of five Bools. Then we pass them into the compress function. the compress function will go through each respective iterable and check the first against the second. If the second has a matching True, then it will be kept. If it's a False, then that item will be dropped. Thus if you study the example above, you will notice that we have a True in the first, third and fourth positions which correspond with A,C and D.

dropwhile(predicate, iterable)

There is a neat little iterator contained in itertools called **dropwhile**. This fun little iterator will drop elements as long as the filter criteria is True. Because of this, you will not see any output from this iterator until the predicate becomes False. This can make the start-up time lengthy, so it's something to be aware of.

Let's look at an example from Python's documentation:

```
1  >>> from itertools import dropwhile
2  >>> list(dropwhile(lambda x: x<5, [1,4,6,4,1]))
3  [6, 4, 1]
```

Here we import **dropwhile** and then we pass it a simple **lambda** statement. This function will return True if **x** is less than 5. Other it will return False. The dropwhile function will loop over the list and pass each element into the lambda. If the lambda returns True, then that value gets dropped. Once we reach the number 6, the lambda returns False and we retain the number 6 and all the values that follow it.

I find it useful to use a regular function over a lambda when I'm learning something new. So let's flip this on its head and create a function that returns True if the number is greater than 5.

```
1  >>> from itertools import dropwhile
2  >>> def greater_than_five(x):
3  ...     return x > 5
4  ...
5  >>> list(dropwhile(greater_than_five, [6, 7, 8, 9, 1, 2, 3, 10]))
6  [1, 2, 3, 10]
```

Here we create a simple function in Python's interpreter. This function is our predicate or filter. If the values we pass to it are True, then they will get dropped. Once we hit a value that is less than 5, then ALL the values after and including that value will be kept, which you can see in the example above.

filterfalse(predicate, iterable)

The **filterfalse** function from itertools is very similar to **dropwhile**. However instead of dropping values that match True, filterfalse will only return those values that evaluated to False. Let's use our function from the previous section to illustrate:

```
1  >>> from itertools import filterfalse
2  >>> def greater_than_five(x):
3  ...     return x > 5
4  ...
5  >>> list(filterfalse(greater_than_five, [6, 7, 8, 9, 1, 2, 3, 10]))
6  [1, 2, 3]
```

Here we pass filterfalse our function and a list of integers. If the integer is less than 5, it is kept. Otherwise it is thrown away. You will notice that our result is only 1, 2 and 3. Unlike dropwhile, filterfalse will check each and every value against our predicate.

groupby(iterable, key=None)

The **groupby** iterator will return consecutive keys and groups from your iterable. This one is kind of hard to wrap your head around without seeing an example. So let's take a look at one! Put the following code into your interpreter or save it in a file:

```
1  from itertools import groupby
2
3  vehicles = [('Ford', 'Taurus'), ('Dodge', 'Durango'),
4             ('Chevrolet', 'Cobalt'), ('Ford', 'F150'),
5             ('Dodge', 'Charger'), ('Ford', 'GT')]
6
7  sorted_vehicles = sorted(vehicles)
8
9  for key, group in groupby(sorted_vehicles, lambda make: make[0]):
10     for make, model in group:
11         print('{model} is made by {make}'.format(model=model,
12                                                   make=make))
13     print ("**** END OF GROUP ***\n")
```

Here we import **groupby** and then create a list of tuples. Then we sort the data so it makes more sense when we output it and it also lets groupby actually group items correctly. Next we actually loop over the iterator returned by groupby which gives us the key and the group. Then we loop over the group and print out what's in it. If you run this code, you should see something like this:

```
1   Cobalt is made by Chevrolet
2   **** END OF GROUP ***
3
4   Charger is made by Dodge
5   Durango is made by Dodge
6   **** END OF GROUP ***
7
8   F150 is made by Ford
9   GT is made by Ford
10  Taurus is made by Ford
11  **** END OF GROUP ***
```

Just for fun, try changing the code such that you pass in **vehicles** instead of **sorted_vehicles**. You will quickly learn why you should sort the data before running it through groupby if you do.

islice(iterable, start, stop)

We actually mentioned **islice** way back in the **count** section. But here we'll look at it a little more in depth. islice is an iterator that returns selected elements from the iterable. That's kind of an opaque statement. Basically what islice does is take a slice by index of your iterable (the thing you iterate over) and returns the selected items as an iterator. There are actually two implementations of islice. There's **itertools.islice(iterable, stop)** and then there's the version of islice that more closely matches regular Python slicing: **islice(iterable, start, stop[, step])**.

Let's look at the first version to see how it works:

```
1   >>> from itertools import islice
2   >>> iterator = islice('123456', 4)
3   >>> next(iterator)
4   '1'
5   >>> next(iterator)
6   '2'
7   >>> next(iterator)
8   '3'
9   >>> next(iterator)
10  '4'
11  >>> next(iterator)
12  Traceback (most recent call last):
13    Python Shell, prompt 15, line 1
14  builtins.StopIteration:
```

In the code above, we pass a string of six characters to islice along with the number 4 which is the stop argument. What this means is that the iterator that islice returns will have the first 4 items from the string in it. We can verify this by calling **next** on our iterator four times, which is what we do above. Python is smart enough to know that if there are only two arguments passed to islice, then the second argument is the **stop** argument.

Let's try giving it three arguments to demonstrate that you can pass it a start and a stop argument. The **count** tool from itertools can help us illustrate this concept:

```
1  >>> from itertools import islice
2  >>> from itertools import count
3  >>> for i in islice(count(), 3, 15):
4  ...        print(i)
5  ...
6  3
7  4
8  5
9  6
10 7
11 8
12 9
13 10
14 11
15 12
16 13
17 14
```

Here we just call count and tell islice to start at the number 3 and stop when we reach 15. It's just like doing a slice except that you are doing it to an iterator and returning a new iterator!

starmap(function, iterable)

The **starmap** tool will create an iterator that can compute using the function and iterable provided. As the documentation mentions, "the difference between map() and starmap() parallels the distinction between function(a,b) and function(*c)."

Let's look at a simple example:

```
1  >>> from itertools import starmap
2  >>> def add(a, b):
3  ...      return a+b
4  ...
5  >>> for item in starmap(add, [(2,3), (4,5)]):
6  ...      print(item)
7  ...
8  5
9  9
```

Here we create a simple adding function that accepts two arguments. Next we create a **for** loop and call **starmap** with the function as its first argument and a list of tuples for the iterable. The starmap function will then pass each tuple element into the function and return an iterator of the results, which we print out.

takewhile(predicate, iterable)

The **takewhile** module is basically the opposite of the **dropwhile** iterator that we looked at earlier. takewhile will create an iterator that returns elements from the iterable only as long as our predicate or filter is True. Let's try a simple example to see how it works:

```
1  >>> from itertools import takewhile
2  >>> list(takewhile(lambda x: x<5, [1,4,6,4,1]))
3  [1, 4]
```

Here we run takewhile using a lambda function and a list. The output is only the first two integers from our iterable. The reason is that 1 and 4 are both less than 5, but 6 is greater. So once takewhile sees the 6, the condition becomes False and it will ignore the rest of the items in the iterable.

tee(iterable, n=2)

The **tee** tool will create *n* iterators from a single iterable. What this means is that you can create multiple iterators from one iterable. Let's look at some explanatory code to how it works:

```
1  >>> from itertools import tee
2  >>> data = 'ABCDE'
3  >>> iter1, iter2 = tee(data)
4  >>> for item in iter1:
5  ...        print(item)
6  ...
7  A
8  B
9  C
10 D
11 E
12 >>> for item in iter2:
13 ...        print(item)
14 ...
15 A
16 B
17 C
18 D
19 E
```

Here we create a 5-letter string and pass it to **tee**. Because tee defaults to 2, we use multiple assignment to acquire the two iterators that are returned from tee. Finally we loop over each of the iterators and print out their contents. As you can see, their content are the same.

zip_longest(*iterables, fillvalue=None)

The **zip_longest** iterator can be used to zip two iterables together. If the iterables don't happen to be the same length, then you can also pass in a **fillvalue**. Let's look at a silly example based on the documentation for this function:

```
1  >>> from itertools import zip_longest
2  >>> for item in zip_longest('ABCD', 'xy', fillvalue='BLANK'):
3  ...        print (item)
4  ...
5  ('A', 'x')
6  ('B', 'y')
7  ('C', 'BLANK')
8  ('D', 'BLANK')
```

In this code we import zip_longest and then pass it two strings to zip together. You will note that the first string is 4-characters long while the second is only 2-characters in length. We also set a fill value of "BLANK". When we loop over this and print it out, you will see that we get tuples returned.

The first two tuples are combinations of the first and second letters from each string respectively. The last two has our fill value inserted.

It should be noted that if the iterable(s) passed to zip_longest have the potential to be infinite, then you should wrap the function with something like islice to limit the number of calls.

The Combinatoric Generators

The itertools library contains four iterators that can be used for creating combinations and permutations of data. We will be covering these fun iterators in this section.

combinations(iterable, r)

If you have the need to create combinations, Python has you covered with **itertools.combinations**. What combinations allows you to do is create an iterator from an iterable that is some length long. Let's take a look:

```
>>> from itertools import combinations
>>> list(combinations('WXYZ', 2))
[('W', 'X'), ('W', 'Y'), ('W', 'Z'), ('X', 'Y'), ('X', 'Z'), ('Y', 'Z')]
```

When you run this, you will notice that combinations returns tuples. To make this output a bit more readable, let's loop over our iterator and join the tuples into a single string:

```
>>> for item in combinations('WXYZ', 2):
...     print(''.join(item))
...
WX
WY
WZ
XY
XZ
YZ
```

Now it's a little easier to see all the various combinations. Note that the combinations function does its combination in lexicographic sort order, so if you the iterable is sorted, then your combination tuples will also be sorted. Also worth noting is that combinations will not produce repeat values in the combinations if all the input elements are unique.

combinations_with_replacement(iterable, r)

The **combinations_with_replacement** with iterator is very similar to **combinations**. The only difference is that it will actually create combinations where elements do repeat. Let's try an example from the previous section to illustrate:

```
1   >>> from itertools import combinations_with_replacement
2   >>> for item in combinations_with_replacement('WXYZ', 2):
3   ...     print(''.join(item))
4   ...
5   WW
6   WX
7   WY
8   WZ
9   XX
10  XY
11  XZ
12  YY
13  YZ
14  ZZ
```

As you can see, we now have four new items in our output: WW, XX, YY and ZZ.

product(*iterables, repeat=1)

The itertools package has a neat little function for creating Cartesian products from a series of input iterables. Yes, that function is **product**. Let's see how it works!

```
1   >>> from itertools import product
2   >>> arrays = [(-1,1), (-3,3), (-5,5)]
3   >>> cp = list(product(*arrays))
4   >>> cp
5   [(-1, -3, -5),
6    (-1, -3, 5),
7    (-1, 3, -5),
8    (-1, 3, 5),
9    (1, -3, -5),
10   (1, -3, 5),
11   (1, 3, -5),
12   (1, 3, 5)]
```

Here we import product and then set up a list of tuples which we assign to the variable **arrays**. Next we call product with those arrays. You will notice that we call it using *arrays. This will cause the list to be "exploded" or applied to the product function in sequence. It means that you are passing in 3 arguments instead of one. If you want, try calling it with the asterisk pre-pended to arrays and see what happens.

permutations

The **permutations** sub-module of itertools will return successive *r* length permutations of elements from the iterable you give it. Much like the combinations function, permutations are emitted in lexicographic sort order. Let's take a look:

```
1  >>> from itertools import permutations
2  >>> for item in permutations('WXYZ', 2):
3  ...     print(''.join(item))
4  ...
5  WX
6  WY
7  WZ
8  XW
9  XY
10 XZ
11 YW
12 YX
13 YZ
14 ZW
15 ZX
16 ZY
```

You will notice that the output it quite a bit longer than the output from combinations. When you use permutations, it will go through all the permutatations of the string, but it won't do repeat values if the input elements are unique.

Wrapping Up

The itertools is a very versatile set of tools for creating iterators. You can use them to create your own iterators all by themselves or in combination with each other. The Python documentation has a lot of great examples that you can study to give you ideas of what can be done with this valuable library.

Chapter 9 - Regular Expressions

Regular expressions are basically a tiny language all their own that you can use inside of Python and many other programming languages. You will often hear regular expressions referred to as "regex", "regexp" or just "RE". Some languages, such as Perl and Ruby, actually support regular expression syntax directly in the language itself. Python only supports them via a library that you need to import. The primary use for regular expressions is matching strings. You create the string matching rules using a regular expression and then you apply it to a string to see if there are any matches.

The regular expression "language" is actually pretty small, so you won't be able to use it for all your string matching needs. Besides that, while there are some tasks that you can use a regular expression for, it may end up so complicated that it becomes difficult to debug. In cases like that, you should just use Python. It should be noted that Python is an excellent language for text parsing in its own right and can be used for anything you do in a regular expression. However, it may take a lot more code to do so and be slower than the regular expression because regular expressions are compiled down and executed in C.

The Matching Characters

When you want to match a character in a string, in most cases you can just use that character or that sub-string. So if we wanted to match "dog", then we would use the letters **dog**. Of course, there are some characters that are reserved for regular expressions. These are known as *metacharacters*. The following is a complete list of the metacharacters that Python's regular expression implementation supports:

    . ^ $ * + ? { } [ ] | ( )

Let's spend a few moments looking at how some of these work. One of the most common pairs of metacharacters you will encounter are the square braces: [and]. There are used for creating a "character class", which is a set of characters that you would like to match on. You may list the characters individually like this: **[xyz]**. This will match any of the characters listed between the braces. You can also use a dash to express a range of characters to match against: **[a-g]**. In this example, we would match against any of the letters a through g.

To actually do a search though, we would need to add a beginning character to look for and an ending character. To make this easier, we can use the asterisk which allows repetitions. Instead of matching *, the * will tell the regular expression that the previous character may be matched zero or more times.

It always helps to see a simple example:

'a[b-f]*f

This regular expression pattern means that we are going to look for the letter *a*, zero or more letters from our class, [b-f] and it needs to end with an *f*. Let's try using this expression in Python:

```
1  >>> import re
2  >>> text = 'abcdfghijk'
3  >>> parser = re.search('a[b-f]*f')
4  <_sre.SRE_Match object; span=(0, 5), match='abcdf'>
5  >>> parser.group()
6  'abcdf'
```

Basically this expression will look at the entire string we pass to it, which in this case is **abcdfghijk**. It will find the *a* at the beginning match against that. Then because it has a character class with an asterisk on the end, it will actually read in the rest of the string to see if it matches. If it doesn't, them it will backtrack one character at a time attempting to find a match.

All this magic happens when we call the **re** module's **search** function. If we don't find a match, then **None** is returned. Otherwise, we will get a **Match** object, which you can see above. To actually see what the match looks like, you need to call the **group** method.

There's another repeating metacharacter which is similar to *. It is +, which will match one or more times. This is a subtle difference from * which matches **zero** or more times. The + requires at least one occurrence of the character it is looking for.

The last two repeating metacharacters work a bit differently. There is the question mark, ?, which will match either once or zero times. It sort of marks the character before it as optional. A simple example would be "co-?op". This would match both "coop" and "co-op".

The final repeated metacharacter is {a,b} where a and b are decimal integers. What this means is that there must be at least a repetitions and at most b. You might want to try out something like this:

xb{1,4}z

This is a pretty silly example, but what it says is that we will match things like **xbz**, **xbbz**, **xbbbz** and **xbbbbz**, but not **xz** because it doesn't have a "b".

The next metacharacter that we'll learn about is ^. This character will allow us to match the characters that are not listed inside our class. In other words, it will complement our class. This will only work if we actually put the ^ inside our class. If it's outside the class, then we will be attempting to actually match against ^. A good example would be something like this: [^a]. This will match any character except the letter 'a'.

The ^ is also used as an anchor in that it is usually used for matches at the beginning of string. There is a corresponding anchor for the end of the string, which is $.

We've spent a lot of time introducing various concepts of regular expressions. In the next few sections, we'll dig into some more real code examples!

Pattern Matching Using search

Let's take a moment to learn some pattern matching basics. When using Python to look for a pattern in a string, you can use the **search** function like we did in the example earlier in this chapter. Here's how:

```python
import re

text = "The ants go marching one by one"

strings = ['the', 'one']

for string in strings:
    match = re.search(string, text)
    if match:
        print('Found "{}" in "{}"'.format(string, text))
        text_pos = match.span()
        print(text[match.start():match.end()])
    else:
        print('Did not find "{}"'.format(string))
```

For this example, we import the **re** module and create a simple string. Then we create a list of two strings that we'll search for in the main string. Next we loop over the strings we plan to search for and actually run a search for them. If there's a match, we print it out. Otherwise we tell the user that the string was not found.

There are a couple of other functions worth explaining in this example. You will notice that we call **span**. This gives us the beginning and ending positions of the string that matched. If you print out the **text_pos** that we assigned the span to, you'll get a tuple like this: (21, 24). Alternatively, you can just call some match methods, which is what we do next. We use **start** and **end** to grab the starting and ending position of the match, which should also be the two numbers that we get from span.

Escape Codes

There are also some sequences that you can search for using special escape codes in Python. Here's a quick list with brief explanations of each:

d   Matches digit

D   Matches non-digit

s   Matches whitespace

S   Matches non-whitespace

w   Matches alphanumeric

W   Matches non-alphanumeric

You can use these escape codes inside of a character class, like so: `[\d]`. This would allow us to find any digit and is the equivalent of `[0-9]`. I highly recommend trying out a few of the others yourself.

Compiling

The re module allows you to "compile" the expressions that you are searching for frequently. This will basically allow you to turn your expression into a **SRE_Pattern** object. You can then use that object in your search function. Let's use the code from earlier and modify it to use compile:

```python
import re

text = "The ants go marching one by one"

strings = ['the', 'one']

for string in strings:
    regex = re.compile(string)
    match = re.search(regex, text)
    if match:
        print('Found "{}" in "{}"'.format(string, text))
        text_pos = match.span()
        print(text[match.start():match.end()])
    else:
        print('Did not find "{}"'.format(string))
```

You will note that here we create our pattern object by calling compile on each string in our list and assigning the result to the variable, **regex**. We then pass that regex to our search function. The rest of the code is the same. The primary reason to use **compile** is to save it to be reused later on in your code. However, compile also takes some flags that can used to enable various special features. We will take a look at that next.

Special Note: When you compile patterns, they will get automatically cached so if you aren't using lot of regular expressions in your code, then you may not need to save the compiled object to a variable.

Compilation Flags

There are 7 compilation flags included in Python 3 that can change how your compiled pattern behaves. Let's go over what each of them do and then we will look at how to use a compilation flag.

re.A / re.ASCII

The ASCII flag tells Python to only match against ASCII instead of using full Unicode matching when coupled with the following escape codes: w, W, b, B, d, D, s and S. There is a re.U / re.UNICODE flag too that is for backwards compatibility purposes; however those flags are redundant since Python 3 already matches in Unicode by default.

re.DEBUG

This will display debug information about your compiled expression.

re.I / re.IGNORECASE

If you'd like to perform case-insensitive matching, then this is the flag for you. If your expression was [a-z] and you compiled it with this flag, your pattern will also match uppercase letters too! This also works for Unicode and it's not affect by the current locale.

re.L / re.LOCALE

Make the escape codes: w, W, b, B, d, D, s and S depend on the current locale. However, the documentation says that you should not depend on this flag because the locale mechanism itself is very unreliable. Instead, just use Unicode matching. The documentation goes on to state that this flag really only makes sense for bytes patterns.

re.M / re.MULTILINE

When you use this flag, you are telling Python to make the ^ pattern character match at both the beginning of the string and at the beginning of each line. It also tells Python that $ should match at the end of the string and the end of each line, which is subtly different from their defaults. See the documentation for additional information.

re.S / re.DOTALL

This fun flag will make the . (period) metacharacter match any character at all. Without the flag, it would match anything except a newline.

re.X / re.VERBOSE

If you find your regular expressions hard to read, then this flag could be just what you need. It will allow to visually separate logical sections of your regular expressions and even add comments! Whitespace within the pattern will be ignored except when in a character class or when the whitespace is preceded by an unescaped backslash.

Using a Compilation Flag

Let's take a moment and look at a simple example that uses the VERBOSE compilation flag! One good example is to take a common email finding regular expression such as r'[w.-]+@[w.-]+' and add some comments using the VERBOSE flag. Let's take a look:

```
1  re.compile('''
2          [\w\.-]+      # the user name
3          @
4          [\w\.-]+'     # the domain
5          ''',
6          re.VERBOSE)
```

Let's move on and learn how to find multiple matches.

Finding Multiple Instances

Up to this point, all we've seen is how to find the first match in a string. But what if you have a string that has multiple matches in it. Let's review how to find a single match:

```
1  >>> import re
2  >>> silly_string = "the cat in the hat"
3  >>> pattern = "the"
4  >>> match = re.search(pattern, text)
5  >>> match.group()
6  'the'
```

Now you can see that there are two instances of the word "the", but we only found one. There are two methods of finding both. The first one that we will look at is the **findall** function:

```
1  >>> import re
2  >>> silly_string = "the cat in the hat"
3  >>> pattern = "the"
4  >>> re.findall(pattern, silly_string)
5  ['the', 'the']
```

The **findall** function will search through the string you pass it and add each match to a list. Once it finishes searching your string, it will return a list of matches. The other way to find multiple matches is to use the **finditer** function.

```
1  import re
2
3  silly_string = "the cat in the hat"
4  pattern = "the"
5
6  for match in re.finditer(pattern, silly_string):
7      s = "Found '{group}' at {begin}:{end}".format(
8          group=match.group(), begin=match.start(),
9          end=match.end())
10     print(s)
```

As you might have guessed, the finditer method returns an iterator of Match instances instead of the strings that you would get from findall. So we needed to do a little formatting of the results before we could print them out. Give this code a try and see how it works.

Backslashes Are Complicated

Backslashes are a bit complicated in Python's regular expressions. The reason being that regular expressions use backslashes to indicate special forms or to allow a special character to be searched for instead of invoking it, such as when we want to search for an dollar sign: $. If we didn't backslash that, we'd just be creating an anchor. The issue comes in because Python uses the backslash character for the same thing in literal strings. Let's say you want to search for a string like this (minus the quotes): "python".

To search for this in a regular expression, you will need to escape the backslash but because Python also uses the backslash, then that backslash also has to be escaped so you'll end up with the following search pattern: "\\python". Fortunately, Python supports raw strings by pre-pending the string with the letter 'r'. So we can make this more readable by doing the following: r"\python".

So if you need to search for something with a backslash, be sure to use raw strings or you may end up with some unexpected results!

Wrapping Up

This chapter barely scratches the surface of all you can do with regular expressions. In fact, there is much more to the module itself. There are entire books on the subject of regular expressions, but this should give you the basics to get started. You will need to search for examples and read the documentation, probably multiple times when you're using regular expressions, but they are a handy tool to have when you need it.

Chapter 10 - The typing Module

Python 3.5 added an interesting new library called **typing**. This adds type hinting to Python. Type hinting is kind of declaring your functions arguments to have a certain type. However the type hinting is not binding. It's just a hint, so there's nothing preventing the programmer from passing something they shouldn't. This is Python after all. You can read the type hinting specification in PEP 484 or you can just read the theory behind it in PEP 483.

Let's take a look at a simple example:

```
1  >>> def some_function(number: int, name: str) -> None:
2          print("%s entered %s" % (name, number))
3
4
5  >>> some_function(13, 'Mike')
6  Mike entered 13
```

This means that **some_function** expects two arguments where the first is an integer and the second is a string. It should also be noted that we have hinted that this function returns None.

Let's back up a bit and write a function the normal way. Then we'll add type hinting to it. In the following example, we have a function that takes list and a name, which in this case would be a string. All it does is check if the name is in the list and returns an appropriate Boolean.

```
1  def process_data(my_list, name):
2      if name in my_list:
3      return True
4      else:
5      return False
6
7  if __name__ == '__main__':
8      my_list = ['Mike', 'Nick', 'Toby']
9      print( process_data(my_list, 'Mike') )
10     print( process_data(my_list, 'John') )
```

Now let's add type hinting to this function:

```
1  def process_data(my_list: list, name: str) -> bool:
2      return name in my_list
3
4  if __name__ == '__main__':
5      my_list = ['Mike', 'Nick', 'Toby']
6      print( process_data(my_list, 'Mike') )
7      print( process_data(my_list, 'John') )
```

In this code we hint that the first argument is a list, the second is a string and the return value is a Boolean.

According to PEP 484, "Type hints may be built-in classes (including those defined in standard library or third-party extension modules), abstract base classes, types available in the types module, and user-defined classes". So that means we can create our own class and add a hint.

```
1  class Fruit:
2      def __init__(self, name, color):
3          self.name = name
4          self.color = color
5
6
7  def salad(fruit_one: Fruit, fruit_two: Fruit) -> list:
8      print(fruit_one.name)
9      print(fruit_two.name)
10     return [fruit_one, fruit_two]
11
12 if __name__ == '__main__':
13     f = Fruit('orange', 'orange')
14     f2 = Fruit('apple', 'red')
15     salad(f, f2)
```

Here we create a simple class and then a function that expects two instances of that class and returns a list object. The other topic that I thought was interesting is that you can create an Alias. Here's a super simple example:

```
1   Animal = str
2
3   def zoo(animal: Animal, number: int) -> None:
4       print("The zoo has %s %s" % (number, animal))
5
6   if __name__ == '__main__':
7       zoo('Zebras', 10)
```

As you may have guessed, we just aliased the **string** type with the variable **Animal**. Then we added a hint to our function using the Animal alias.

Type Hints and Overloaded Functions

One obvious place in your code that I think Type Hints would work great in are overloaded functions. We learned about function overloads back in Chapter 4. Let's grab the overloaded adding function from that chapter and take a look at how much better it will be with type hints. Here's the original code:

```
1   from functools import singledispatch
2
3
4   @singledispatch
5   def add(a, b):
6       raise NotImplementedError('Unsupported type')
7
8
9   @add.register(int)
10  def _(a, b):
11      print("First argument is of type ", type(a))
12      print(a + b)
13
14
15  @add.register(str)
16  def _(a, b):
17      print("First argument is of type ", type(a))
18      print(a + b)
19
20
21  @add.register(list)
22  def _(a, b):
23      print("First argument is of type ", type(a))
24      print(a + b)
```

This example's first argument is pretty obvious if you understand how Python's function overloads work. But what we don't know is what the second argument is supposed to be. We can infer it, but in Python it is almost always best to be explicit rather than implicit. So let's add some type hints:

```python
from functools import singledispatch


@singledispatch
def add(a, b):
    raise NotImplementedError('Unsupported type')


@add.register(int)
def _(a: int, b: int) -> int:
    print("First argument is of type ", type(a))
    print(a + b)
    return a + b


@add.register(str)
def _(a: str, b: str) -> str:
    print("First argument is of type ", type(a))
    print(a + b)
    return a + b


@add.register(list)
def _(a: list, b: list) -> list:
    print("First argument is of type ", type(a))
    print(a + b)
    return a + b
```

Now that we've added some type hints, we can tell just by looking at the function definition what the arguments should be. Before type hints were added, you would have needed to mention the argument types in the function's docstring, but because we have these handy hints, we don't need to clutter our docstring with that kind of information any longer.

I have worked with some poorly documented Python code before and even if it only had type hints in the function and method definitions the code would have been much easier to figure out. Type hints aren't a replacement for good documentation, but they do enhance our ability to understand our code in the future.

Wrapping Up

When I first heard about type hinting, I was intrigued. It's a neat concept and I can definitely see uses for it. The first use case that springs to my mind is just self-documenting your code. I've worked on too many code bases where it's difficult to tell what a function or class accepts and while type hinting doesn't enforce anything, it would certainly bring some clarity to some of that ambiguous code. It would be neat if some Python IDEs added an optional flag that could check your code's type hints and make sure you're calling your code correctly too.

I highly recommend checking out the official documentation as there's a lot more information there. The PEPs also contain a lot of good details. Have fun and happy coding!

Part II - Odds and Ends

There are always valuable topics that need to be covered but don't really fit into any specific section. This is why I have a section that's just devoted to those kinds of topics, which I lovingly refer to as "odds and ends". In this section, we will focus on Python built-ins, what is unicode and why do we care, benchmarking, encryption, databases, descriptors and scope rules in Python.

Here's a chapter-by-chapter listing:

- Chapter 11 - map, filter and more
- Chapter 12 - unicode
- Chapter 13 - benchmarking
- Chapter 14 - encryption
- Chapter 15 - Connecting to databases
- Chapter 16 - super
- Chapter 17 - descriptors (magic methods)
- Chapter 18 - Scope (local, global and the new non_local)

These topics will help you understand your craft that much better and hopefully give you some good points of reference for your future work. Let's start learning!

Chapter 11 - Python Built-ins

Built-ins are a somewhat overlooked part of Python. You use them every day, but there are a number of them that get overlooked or just aren't used to their full potential. This chapter won't be covering all the built-ins in Python, but will focus on the ones that you probably don't use every day.

any

The **any** built-in accepts an iterable and will return True is any element in said iterable is True. Let's take a look at an example:

```
1  >>> any([0,0,0,1])
2  True
```

In this case, we pass **any** a list of zeros and a one. Because there's a one there, it returns True. You might be wondering when you would ever use this built-in. I did too at first. An example that cropped up in one of my jobs involved a very complex user iterface where I had to test various pieces of functionality. One of the items that I needed to test was if a certain list of widgets had been shown or enabled when they shouldn't be. The any built-in was very useful for that.

Here's an example that kind of demonstrates what I'm talking about, although it's not the actual code I used:

```
1  >>> widget_one = ''
2  >>> widget_two = ''
3  >>> widget_three = 'button'
4  >>> widgets_exist = any([widget_one, widget_two, widget_three])
5  >>> widgets_exist
6  True
```

Basically I would query the user iterface and ask it if widgets one through three existed and put the responses into a list. If any of them returned True, then I'd raise an error.

You might want to check out Python's **all** built-in as it has similar functionality except that it will only return True if every single item in the iterable is True.

enumerate

Have you ever needed to loop over a list *and* also needed to know where in the list you were at? You could add a counter that you increment as you loop, or you could use Python's built-in **enumerate** function! Let's try it out on a string!

```
1  >>> my_string = 'abcdefg'
2  >>> for pos, letter in enumerate(my_string):
3  ...      print (pos, letter)
4  ...
5  0 a
6  1 b
7  2 c
8  3 d
9  4 e
10 5 f
11 6 g
```

In this example, we have a 6-letter string. You will notice that in our loop, we wrap the string in a call to **enumerate**. This returns the position of each item in the iterable as well as the value. We print them both out so you can see what's going on. I personally have found many use cases for enumerate. I'm sure you will too.

eval

The **eval** built-in is fairly controversial in the Python community. The reason for this is that eval accepts strings and basically runs them. If you were to allow users to input any string to be parsed and evaluated by eval, then you just created a major security breach. However, if the code that uses eval cannot be interacted with by the user and only by the developer, then it is okay to use. Some will argue that it's still not safe, but if you have a rogue developer, they can do a lot more harm doing other things than using eval.

Let's take a look at a simple example:

```
1  >>> var = 10
2  >>> source = 'var * 2'
3  >>> eval(source)
4  20
```

As you can see, we create two variables. The first is assigned the integer 10. The second has a string that has the same letters as the variable we just defined and it looks like we're going to multiply it by two. However it's just a string so it doesn't do anything. But with eval, we can make it do something! You can see it in action on the very next line where we pass the string into eval and we get a result. This is why people think that eval can be dangerous.

There is another built-in function called **exec** which supports the dynamic execution of Python code. It's a somewhat "dangerous" built-in too, but it doesn't have the bad reputation that eval does. It's a neat little tool, but use it with caution.

filter

The **filter** built-in function will take a function and an iterable and return an iterator for those elements within the iterable for which the passed in function returns True. That statement sounds a bit confusing to read, so let's look at an example:

```
1  >>> def less_than_ten(x):
2  ...     return x < 10
3  ...
4  >>> my_list = [1, 2, 3, 10, 11, 12]
5  >>> for item in filter(less_than_ten, my_list):
6  ...     print(item)
7  ...
8  1
9  2
10 3
```

Here we create a simple function that tests if the integer we pass to it is less than 10. If it is, then it returns True; otherwise it returns False. Next we create a list of 6 integers with half of them being less than 10. Finally we use **filter** to filter out the integers that are greater than ten and only print the ones that are less.

You may recall that the itertools module has a function that is similar to this one called **filterfalse**. That function is the opposite of this one and only returns elements of the iterable when the function returns False.

map

The **map** built-in also takes a function and an iterable and return an iterator that applies the function to each item in the iterable. Let's take a look at a simple example:

```
1  >>> def doubler(x):
2  ...     return x * 2
3  ...
4  >>> my_list = [1, 2, 3, 4, 5]
5  >>> for item in map(doubler, my_list):
6  ...     print(item)
7  ...
8  2
9  4
10 6
11 8
12 10
```

The first thing we define is a function that will double whatever is passed to it. Next we have a list of integers, 1-5. Finally we create a for loop that loops over the iterator that is returned when we call map with our function and list. The code inside the loop will print out the results.

The map and filter functions basically duplicate the features of generator expressions in Python 3. In Python 2, they duplicate the functionality of list comprehensions. We could shorten the code above a bit and make it return a list like so:

```
1  >>> list(map(doubler, my_list))
2  [2, 4, 6, 8, 10]
```

But you can do the same thing with a list comprehension:

```
1  >>> [doubler(x) for x in my_list]
2  [2, 4, 6, 8, 10]
```

So it's really up to you which you want to use.

zip

The **zip** built-in takes a series of iterables and aggregates the elements from each of them. Let's see what that means:

```
1  >>> keys = ['x', 'y', 'z']
2  >>> values = [5, 6, 7]
3  >>> zip(keys, values)
4  <zip object at 0x7fc76575a548>
5  >>> list(zip(keys, values))
6  [('x', 5), ('y', 6), ('z', 7)]
```

In this example, we have two lists of equal size. Next we zip them together with the zip function. This just returns a zip object, so we wrap that in a call to the **list** built-in to see what the result is. We end up with a list of tuples. You can see here that zip matched up the items in each list by position and put them into tuples.

One of the most popular use cases for zip it to take two lists and turn them into a dictionary:

```
1  >>> keys = ['x', 'y', 'z']
2  >>> values = [5, 6, 7]
3  >>> my_dict = dict(zip(keys, values))
4  >>> my_dict
5  {'x': 5, 'y': 6, 'z': 7}
```

When you pass a series of tuples to Python's **dict** built-in, it will create a dictionary as you can see above. I've used this technique from time to time in my own code.

Wrapping Up

While this was a brief tour, I hope it gave you a good idea of just how much power Python's built-ins give you. There are many others that you use every day, such as list, dict and dir. The built-in functions that you learned about in this chapter probably won't get used every day, but they can be extremely helpful in certain situations. I am actually devoting an entire chapter to a special built-in known as **super**, which you can read about later on in the book. Have fun with these and be sure to look up the documentation to see what other jewels exist.

Chapter 12 - Unicode

One of the major changes in Python 3 was the move to make all strings Unicode. Previously, there was a **str** type and a **unicode** type. For example:

```
1  # Python 2
2  >>> x = 'blah'
3  >>> type(x)
4  str
5  >>> y = u'blah'
6  >>> type(y)
7  unicode
```

If we do the same thing in Python 3, you will note that it always returns a string type:

```
1  # Python 3
2  >>> x = 'blah'
3  >>> type(x)
4  <class 'str'>
5  >>> y = u'blah'
6  >>> type(y)
7  <class 'str'>
```

Python 3 defaults to the UTF-8 encoding. What all this means is that you can now use Unicode characters in your strings and for variable names. Let's see how this works in practice:

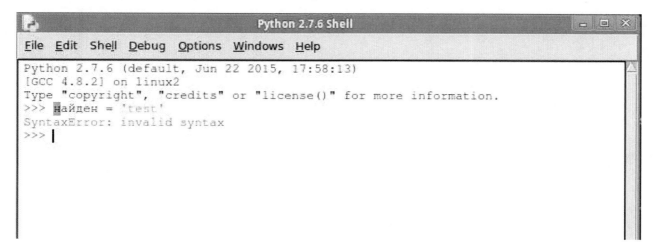

For this example, we tried to open a file that didn't exist and pretended we were in Russia. When the file wasn't found, we caught the error and printed out the error message in Russian. Note that I used Google Translate for this example, so the wording might be a little off.

Let's try creating a unicode variable name in Python 2:

Python 2 will throw a **SyntaxError** when we try to use Unicode in our variable name. Now let's see how Python 3 handles it:

```
Python 3.5.1+ Shell
File  Edit  Shell  Debug  Options  Window  Help
Python 3.5.1+ (default, Mar 30 2016, 22:46:26)
[GCC 5.3.1 20160330] on linux
Type "copyright", "credits" or "license()" for more information.
>>> найден = 'test'
>>> print(найден)
test
>>>
```

Unicode variable names work just fine in the latest Python. In Python 2, I was always running into oddball issues when I would read a file or web page that wasn't in ASCII. An example that you might see in your output might look something like this:

```
1  # Python 2
2  >>> 'abcdef' + chr(255)
3  'abcdef\xff'
```

Note that the end of that string has some funny characters there. That should be a "☒" instead of xff, which is basically a hex version of the character. In Python 3 you will get what you expect:

```
1  # Python 3
2  >>> 'abcdef' + chr(255)
3  'abcdef☐'
```

One thing I was always tempted to try to fix this issue in Python 2 was to wrap the call in Python's built-in unicode function. It's supposed to cast a string to Unicode after all. What could go wrong? Let's find out!

```
1  # Python 2
2  >>> unicode('abcdef' + chr(255))
3  Traceback (most recent call last):
4    File "<pyshell#1>", line 1, in <module>
5      unicode('abcdef' + chr(255))
6  UnicodeDecodeError: 'ascii' codec can't decode byte 0xff in position 6: ordinal \
7  not in range(128)
```

The **UnicodeDecodeError** exception can be a royal pain in Python 2. I know I spent hours fighting it on certain projects. I look forward to not having to deal with those kinds of issues so much in Python 3. I will note that there is a handy package on the Python Packing Index called Unidecode that can take most Unicode characters and turn them into ASCII. I have resorted to using that in the past to fix certain issues with input.

Encoding / Decoding

Back in the good ol' days, you quickly learned that you cannot decode a unicode string and you cannot encode a str type either. If you tried to take a unicode string and decode it to ascii (i.e. convert it to a byte string), you would get a UnicodeEncodeError. For example:

```
1  >>> u"\xa0".decode("ascii")
2
3  Traceback (most recent call last):
4    File "<pyshell#1>", line 1, in <module>
5      u"\xa0".decode("ascii")
6  UnicodeEncodeError: 'ascii' codec can't encode character u'\xa0' in position 0: \
7  ordinal not in range(128)
```

If you tried something like this in Python 3, you would get an **AttributeError**

```
1  >>> u"\xa0".decode("ascii")
2  Traceback (most recent call last):
3    Python Shell, prompt 11, line 1
4  builtins.AttributeError: 'str' object has no attribute 'decode'
```

The reason is pretty obvious in that strings in Python 3 don't have the decode attribute. However, byte strings do! Let's try a byte string instead:

```
1  >>> b"\xa0".decode("ascii")
2  Traceback (most recent call last):
3    Python Shell, prompt 15, line 1
4  builtins.UnicodeDecodeError: 'ascii' codec can't decode byte 0xa0 in position
```

That still didn't quite work the way we wanted as the ASCII codec didn't know how to handle the character we passed to it. Fortunately you can pass extra parameters to the decode method and make this work:

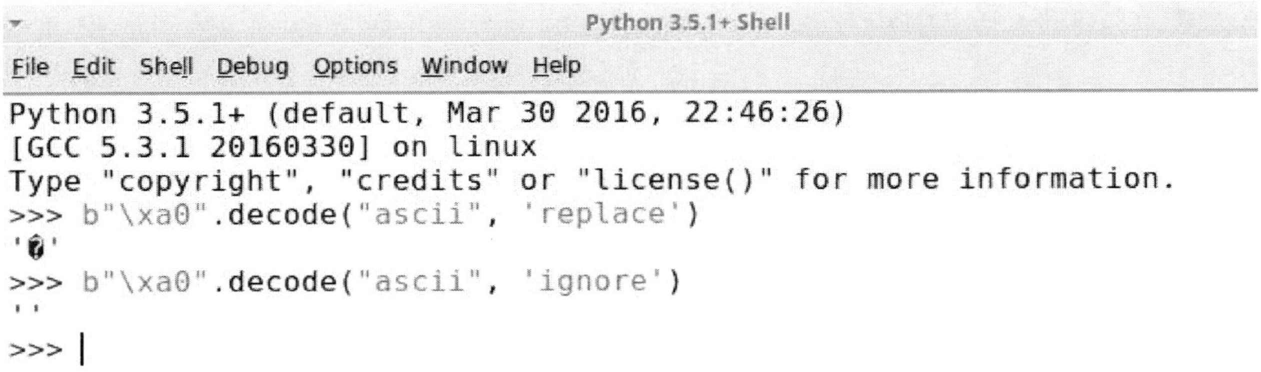

```
Python 3.5.1+ Shell

File  Edit  Shell  Debug  Options  Window  Help

Python 3.5.1+ (default, Mar 30 2016, 22:46:26)
[GCC 5.3.1 20160330] on linux
Type "copyright", "credits" or "license()" for more information.
>>> b"\xa0".decode("ascii", 'replace')
'�'
>>> b"\xa0".decode("ascii", 'ignore')
''
>>>
```

This example shows what happens if you tell the decode method to replace the character or to just ignore it. You can see the results for yourself.

Now let's look at an example from the Python documentation to learn how to encode a string.

```
1   >>> u = chr(40960) + 'abcd' + chr(1972)
2   >>> u
3   'ꘀabcd\u07b4'
4   >>> u.encode('ascii')
5   Traceback (most recent call last):
6     Python Shell, prompt 20, line 1
7   builtins.UnicodeEncodeError: 'ascii' codec can't encode character '\ua000' in po\
8   sition 0: ordinal not in range(128)
9   >>> u.encode('ascii', 'ignore')
10  b'abcd'
11  >>> u.encode('ascii', 'replace')
12  b'?abcd?'
```

For this example, we took a string and added a non-ASCII character to the beginning and the end of the string. Then we tried to convert the string to a bytes representation of the Unicode string using the encode method. The first attempt did not work and gave us an error. The next one used the **ignore** flag, which basically removed the non-ASCII characters from the string entirely. The last example uses the **replace** flag which just puts question marks in place for the unknown Unicode characters.

If you need to work with encodings a lot, Python also has a module called **codecs** that you should check out.

Wrapping Up

At this point you should know enough about Unicode to actually use it. Unicode makes it possible for your application to support other languages both in the code itself and in its output. You have also just scratched the surface on how to encode and decode strings in Python. The documentation on this subject is pretty extensive, so if you need more information, please check it out.

Chapter 13 - Benchmarking

What does it mean to benchmark ones code? The main idea behind benchmarking or profiling is to figure out how fast your code executes and where the bottlenecks are. The main reason to do this sort of thing is for optimization. You will run into situations where you need your code to run faster because your business needs have changed. When this happens, you will need to figure out what parts of your code are slowing it down.

This chapter will only cover how to profile your code using a variety of tools. It will not go into actually optimizing your code. Let's get started!

timeit

Python comes with a module called **timeit**. You can use it to time small code snippets. The timeit module uses platform-specific time functions so that you will get the most accurate timings possible.

The timeit module has a command line interface, but it can also be imported. We will start out by looking at how to use timeit from the command line. Open up a terminal and try the following examples:

> python -m timeit -s "[ord(x) for x in 'abcdfghi']" 100000000 loops, best of 3: 0.0115 usec per loop
>
> python -m timeit -s "[chr(int(x)) for x in '123456789']" 100000000 loops, best of 3: 0.0119 usec per loop

What's going on here? Well, when you call Python on the command line and pass it the "-m" option, you are telling it to look up a module and use it as the main program. The "-s" tells the timeit module to run setup once. Then it runs the code for n number of loops 3 times and returns the best average of the 3 runs. For these silly examples, you won't see much difference.

Your output will likely be slightly different as it is dependent on your computer's specifications.

Let's write a silly function and see if we can time it from the command line:

```
1   # simple_func.py
2   def my_function():
3       try:
4           1 / 0
5       except ZeroDivisionError:
6           pass
```

All this function does is cause an error that is promptly ignored. Yes, it's another silly example. To get timeit to run this code on the command line, we will need to import the code into its namespace, so make sure you have changed your current working directory to be in the same folder that this script is in. Then run the following:

> python -m timeit "import simple_func; simple_func.my_function()" 1000000 loops, best of 3: 1.77 usec per loop

Here we import the function and then call it. Note that we separate the import and the function call with semi-colons and that the Python code is in quotes. Now we're ready to learn how to use timeit inside an actual Python script.

Importing timeit for Testing

Using the timeit module inside your code is also pretty easy. We'll use the same silly script from before and show you how below:

```
1   # simple_func2.py
2   def my_function():
3       try:
4           1 / 0
5       except ZeroDivisionError:
6           pass
7
8   if __name__ == "__main__":
9       import timeit
10      setup = "from __main__ import my_function"
11      print(timeit.timeit("my_function()", setup=setup))
```

Here we check to see if the script is being run directly (i.e. not imported). If it is, then we import timeit, create a setup string to import the function into timeit's namespace and then we call timeit.timeit. You will note that we pass a call to the function in quotes, then the setup string. And that's really all there is to it! Now let's learn about how to write our own timer decorator.

Use a decorator

Writing your own timer is a lot of fun too, although it may not be as accurate as just using timeit depending on the use case. Regardless, we're going to write our own custom function timing decorator! Here's the code:

```python
import random
import time

def timerfunc(func):
    """
    A timer decorator
    """
    def function_timer(*args, **kwargs):
        """
        A nested function for timing other functions
        """
        start = time.time()
        value = func(*args, **kwargs)
        end = time.time()
        runtime = end - start
        msg = "The runtime for {func} took {time} seconds to complete"
        print(msg.format(func=func.__name__,
                         time=runtime))
        return value
    return function_timer


@timerfunc
def long_runner():
    for x in range(5):
        sleep_time = random.choice(range(1,5))
        time.sleep(sleep_time)

if __name__ == '__main__':
    long_runner()
```

For this example, we import the **random** and the **time** modules from Python's standard library. Then we create our decorator function. You will notice that it accepts a function and has another function inside of it. The nested function will grab the time before calling the passed in function. Then it waits for the function to return and grabs the end time. Now we know how long the function took to run, so we print it out. Of course, the decorator also needs to return the result of the function call and the function itself, so that's what the last two statements are all about.

The next function is decorated with our timing decorator. You will note that it uses random to "randomly" sleep a few seconds. This is just to demonstrate a long running program. You would actually want to time functions that connect to databases (or run large queries), websites, run threads or do other things that take a while to complete.

Each time you run this code, the result will be slightly different. Give it a try and see for yourself!

Create a Timing Context Manager

Some programmers like to use context managers to time small pieces of code. So let's create our own timer context manager class!

```python
1   import random
2   import time
3
4   class MyTimer():
5
6       def __init__(self):
7           self.start = time.time()
8
9       def __enter__(self):
10          return self
11
12      def __exit__(self, exc_type, exc_val, exc_tb):
13          end = time.time()
14          runtime = end - self.start
15          msg = 'The function took {time} seconds to complete'
16          print(msg.format(time=runtime))
17
18
19  def long_runner():
20      for x in range(5):
21          sleep_time = random.choice(range(1,5))
22          time.sleep(sleep_time)
23
24
25  if __name__ == '__main__':
26      with MyTimer():
27          long_runner()
```

In this example, we use the class's __init__ method to start our timer. The __enter__ method doesn't need to do anything other then return itself. Lastly, the __exit__ method has all the juicy bits. Here we grab the end time, calculate the total run time and print it out.

The end of the code actually shows an example of using our context manager where we wrap the function from the previous example in our custom context manager.

cProfile

Python comes with its own code profilers built-in. There is the **profile** module and the **cProfile** module. The profile module is pure Python, but it will add a lot of overhead to anything you profile, so it's usually recommended that you go with cProfile, which has a similar interface but is much faster.

We're not going to go into a lot of detail about this module in this chapter, but let's look at a couple of fun examples so you get a taste for what it can do.

```
1  >>> import cProfile
2  >>> cProfile.run("[x for x in range(1500)]")
3          4 function calls in 0.001 seconds
4
5     Ordered by: standard name
6
7     ncalls  tottime  percall  cumtime  percall filename:lineno(function)
8          1    0.000    0.000    0.000    0.000 <string>:1(<listcomp>)
9          1    0.000    0.000    0.000    0.000 <string>:1(<module>)
10         1    0.001    0.001    0.001    0.001 {built-in method builtins.exec}
11         1    0.000    0.000    0.000    0.000 {method 'disable' of '_lsprof.Prof\
12  iler' objects}
```

Let's break this down a bit. The first line shows that there were 4 function calls. The next line tells us how the results are ordered. According to the documentation, standard name refers to the far right column. There are a number of columns here.

- **ncalls** is the number of calls made.
- **tottime** is a total of the time spent in the given function.
- **percall** refers to the quotient of tottime divided by ncalls
- **cumtime** is the cumulative time spent in this and all subfunctions. It's even accurate for recursive functions!
- The second **percall** column is the quotient of cumtime divided by primitive calls
- **filename:lineno(function)** provides the respective data of each function

You can call cProfile on the command line in much the same way as we did with the timeit module. The main difference is that you would pass a Python script to it instead of just passing a snippet. Here's an example call:

```
1  python -m cProfile test.py
```

Give it a try on one of your own modules or try it on one of Python's modules to see how it works.

line_profiler

There's a neat 3rd party project called **line_profiler** that is designed to profile the time each individual line takes to execute. It also includes a script called **kernprof** for profiling Python applications and scripts using line_profiler. Just use pip to install the package. Here's how:

```
1  pip install line_profiler
```

To actually use the line_profiler, we will need some code to profile. But first, I need to explain how line_profiler works when you call it on the command line. You will actually be calling line_profiler by calling the kernprof script. I thought that was a bit confusing the first time I used it, but that's just the way it works. Here's the normal way to use it:

```
1  kernprof -l silly_functions.py
```

This will print out the following message when it finishes: *Wrote profile results to silly_functions.py.lprof*. This is a binary file that we can't view directly. When we run kernprof though, it will actually inject an instance of **LineProfiler** into your script's **__builtins__** namespace. The instance will be named **profile** and is meant to be used as a decorator. With that in mind, we can actually write our script:

```
1   # silly_functions.py
2   import time
3
4   @profile
5   def fast_function():
6       print("I'm a fast function!")
7
8   @profile
9   def slow_function():
10      time.sleep(2)
11      print("I'm a slow function")
12
13  if __name__ == '__main__':
14      fast_function()
15      slow_function()
```

So now we have two decorated functions that are decorated with something that isn't imported. If you actually try to run this script as is, you will get a **NameError** because "profile" is not defined. So always remember to remove your decorators after you have profiled your code!

Let's back up and learn how to actually view the results of our profiler. There are two methods we can use. The first is to use the line_profiler module to read our results file:

```
python -m line_profiler silly_functions.py.lprof
```

The alternate method is to just use kernprof in verbose mode by passing is -**v**:

```
kernprof -l -v silly_functions.py
```

Regardless which method you use, you should end up seeing something like the following get printed to your screen:

```
I'm a fast function!
I'm a slow function
Wrote profile results to silly_functions.py.lprof
Timer unit: 1e-06 s

Total time: 3.4e-05 s
File: silly_functions.py
Function: fast_function at line 3

Line #      Hits         Time  Per Hit   % Time  Line Contents
==============================================================
     3                                           @profile
     4                                           def fast_function():
     5         1           34     34.0    100.0       print("I'm a fast function!\
")

Total time: 2.001 s
File: silly_functions.py
Function: slow_function at line 7

Line #      Hits         Time  Per Hit   % Time  Line Contents
==============================================================
     7                                           @profile
     8                                           def slow_function():
     9         1      2000942 2000942.0    100.0       time.sleep(2)
    10         1           59     59.0      0.0       print("I'm a slow function")
```

You will notice that the source code is printed out with the timing information for each line. There are six columns of information here. Let's find out what each one means.

- **Line #** - The line number of the code that was profiled
- **Hits** - The number of times that particular line was executed
- **Time** - The total amount of time the line took to execute (in the timer's unit). The timer unit can be seen at the beginning of the output
- **Per Hit** - The average amount of time that line of code took to execute (in timer units)
- **% Time** - The percentage of time spent on the line relative to the total amount of time spent in said function
- **Line Contents** - The actual source code that was executed

If you happen to be an IPython user, then you might want to know that IPython has a magic command (%lprun) that allows you to specify functions to profile and even which statement to execute.

memory_profiler

Another great 3rd party profiling package is **memory_profiler**. The memory_profiler module can be used for monitoring memory consumption in a process or you can use it for a line-by-line analysis of the memory consumption of your code. Since it's not included with Python, we'll have to install it. You can use pip for this:

```
1  pip install memory_profiler
```

Once it's installed, we need some code to run it against. The memory_profiler actually works in much the same way as line_profiler in that when you run it, memory_profiler will inject an instance of itself into __builtins__ named profile that you are supposed to use as a decorator on the function you are profiling. Here's a simple example:

```
1  # memo_prof.py
2  @profile
3  def mem_func():
4      lots_of_numbers = list(range(1500))
5      x = ['letters'] * (5 ** 10)
6      del lots_of_numbers
7      return None
8
9  if __name__ == '__main__':
10      mem_func()
```

In this example, we create a list that contains 1500 integers. Then we create a list with 9765625 (5 to the 10 power) instances of a string. Finally we delete the first list and return. The memory_profiler doesn't have another script you need to run to do the actual profiling like line_profiler did. Instead you can just run Python and use its -**m** parameter on the command line to load the module and run it against our script:

```
python -m memory_profiler memo_prof.py
Filename: memo_prof.py

Line #    Mem usage    Increment   Line Contents
================================================
     1    16.672 MiB    0.000 MiB   @profile
     2                              def mem_func():
     3    16.707 MiB    0.035 MiB       lots_of_numbers = list(range(1500))
     4    91.215 MiB   74.508 MiB       x = ['letters'] * (5 ** 10)
     5    91.215 MiB    0.000 MiB       del lots_of_numbers
     6    91.215 MiB    0.000 MiB       return None
```

The columns are pretty self-explanatory this time around. We have our line numbers and then the amount of memory used after said line was executed. Next we have an increment field which tells us the difference in memory of the current line versus the line previous. The very last column is for the code itself.

The memory_profiler also includes **mprof** which can be used to create full memory usage reports over time instead of line-by-line. It's very easy to use; just take a look:

```
$ mprof run memo_prof.py
mprof: Sampling memory every 0.1s
running as a Python program...
```

mprof can also create a graph that shows you how your application consumed memory over time. To get the graph, all you need to do is:

```
$ mprof plot
```

For the silly example we created earlier, I got the following graph:

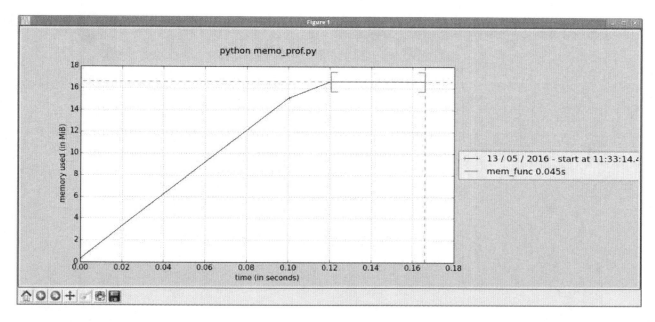

You should try running it yourself against a much more complex example to see a more interesting plot.

profilehooks

The last 3rd party package that we will look at in this chapter is called **profilehooks**. It is a collection of decorators specifically designed for profiling functions. To install profilehooks, just do the following:

```
1   pip install profilehooks
```

Now that we have it installed, let's re-use the example from the last section and modify it slightly to use profilehooks:

```
1   # profhooks.py
2   from profilehooks import profile
3
4
5   @profile
6   def mem_func():
7       lots_of_numbers = list(range(1500))
8       x = ['letters'] * (5 ** 10)
9       del lots_of_numbers
10      return None
11
```

```
12  if __name__ == '__main__':
13      mem_func()
```

All you need to do to use profilehooks is import it and then decorate the function that you want to profile. If you run the code above, you will get output similar to the following sent to stdout:

```
● ● ●                    chapter13_benchmarking — -bash — 95×24
Mikes-MacBook-Pro:chapter13_benchmarking michael$ python3 profhooks.py

*** PROFILER RESULTS ***
mem_func (profhooks.py:5)
function called 1 times

        2 function calls in 0.045 seconds

   Ordered by: cumulative time, internal time, call count

   ncalls  tottime  percall  cumtime  percall filename:lineno(function)
        1    0.045    0.045    0.045    0.045 profhooks.py:5(mem_func)
        1    0.000    0.000    0.000    0.000 {method 'disable' of '_lsprof.Profiler' objects}
        0    0.000             0.000          profile:0(profiler)


Mikes-MacBook-Pro:chapter13_benchmarking michael$
```

The output for this package appears to follow that of the cProfile module from Python's standard library. You can refer to the descriptions of the columns earlier in this chapter to see what these mean. The profilehooks package has two more decorators. The first one we will look at is called **timecall**. It gives us the course run time of the function:

```
1   # profhooks2.py
2   from profilehooks import timecall
3
4   @timecall
5   def mem_func():
6       lots_of_numbers = list(range(1500))
7       x = ['letters'] * (5 ** 10)
8       del lots_of_numbers
9       return None
10
11  if __name__ == '__main__':
12      mem_func()
```

When you run this piece of code, you will see something similar to the following output:

```
1  mem_func (c:\path_to_script\profhooks2.py:3):
2    0.141 seconds
```

All decorator does is time the execution time of the function but without the overhead of profiling. It's kind of like using **timeit**.

The last decorator that profhooks provides is called **coverage**. It is supposed to print out the line coverage of a single function. I didn't really find this one all that useful myself, but you're welcome to give it a try on your own.

Finally I just want to mention that you can also run profilehooks on the command line using Python's -m flag:

```
1  python -m profilehooks mymodule.py
```

The profilehooks package is pretty new, but I think it has some potential.

Wrapping Up

We covered a lot of information in this chapter. You learned how to use Python's built-in modules, timeit and cProfile to time and profile your code, respectively. You also learned how to write your own timing code and use it as a decorator or a context manager. Then we moved on and looked at some 3rd party packages; namely **line_profiler**, **memory_profiler** and **profilehooks**. At this point, you should be well on your way to benchmarking your own code. Give it a try and see if you can find any bottlenecks of your own.

Chapter 14 - Encryption and Cryptography

Python doesn't have very much in its standard library that deals with encryption. Instead, you get hashing libraries. We'll take a brief look at those in the chapter, but the primary focus will be on the following 3rd party packages: PyCrypto and cryptography. We will learn how to encrypt and decrypt strings with both of these libraries.

Hashing

If you need secure hashes or message digest algorithms, then Python's standard library has you covered in the **hashlib** module. It includes the FIPS secure hash algorithms SHA1, SHA224, SHA256, SHA384, and SHA512 as well as RSAâ€™s MD5 algorithm. Python also supports the adler32 and crc32 hash functions, but those are in the **zlib** module.

One of the most popular uses of hashes is storing the hash of a password instead of the password itself. Of course, the hash has to be a good one or it can be decrypted. Another popular use case for hashes is to hash a file and then send the file and its hash separately. Then the person receiving the file can run a hash on the file to see if it matches the hash that was sent. If it does, then that means no one has changed the file in transit.

Let's try creating an md5 hash:

```
1  >>> import hashlib
2  >>> md5 = hashlib.md5()
3  >>> md5.update('Python rocks!')
4  Traceback (most recent call last):
5    File "<pyshell#5>", line 1, in <module>
6      md5.update('Python rocks!')
7  TypeError: Unicode-objects must be encoded before hashing
8  >>> md5.update(b'Python rocks!')
9  >>> md5.digest()
10 b'\x14\x82\xec\x1b#d\xf6N}\x16*+[\x16\xf4w'
```

Let's take a moment to break this down a bit. First off, we import **hashlib** and then we create an instance of an md5 HASH object. Next we add some text to the hash object and we get a traceback. It turns out that to use the md5 hash, you have to pass it a byte string instead of a regular string. So we try that and then call it's **digest** method to get our hash. If you prefer the hex digest, we can do that too:

```
1  >>> md5.hexdigest()
2  '1482ec1b2364f64e7d162a2b5b16f477'
```

There's actually a shortcut method of creating a hash, so we'll look at that next when we create our sha512 hash:

```
1  >>> sha = hashlib.sha1(b'Hello Python').hexdigest()
2  >>> sha
3  '422fbfbc67fe17c86642c5eaaa48f8b670cbed1b'
```

As you can see, we can create our hash instance and call its digest method at the same time. Then we print out the hash to see what it is. I chose to use the sha1 hash as it has a nice short hash that will fit the page better. But it's also less secure, so feel free to try one of the others.

Key Derivation

Python has pretty limited support for key derivation built into the standard library. In fact, the only method that hashlib provides is the **pbkdf2_hmac** method, which is the PKCS#5 password-based key derivation function 2. It uses HMAC as its psuedorandom function. You might use something like this for hashing your password as it supports a salt and iterations. For example, if you were to use SHA-256 you would need a salt of at least 16 bytes and a minimum of 100,000 iterations.

As a quick aside, a salt is just random data that you use as additional input into your hash to make it harder to "unhash" your password. Basically it protects your password from dictionary attacks and pre-computed rainbow tables.

Let's look at a simple example:

```
1  >>> import binascii
2  >>> dk = hashlib.pbkdf2_hmac(hash_name='sha256',
3          password=b'bad_password34',
4          salt=b'bad_salt',
5          iterations=100000)
6  >>> binascii.hexlify(dk)
7  b'6e97bad21f6200f9087036a71e7ca9fa01a59e1d697f7e0284cd7f9b897d7c02'
```

Here we create a SHA256 hash on a password using a lousy salt but with 100,000 iterations. Of course, SHA is not actually recommended for creating keys of passwords. Instead you should use something like **scrypt** instead. Another good option would be the 3rd party package, bcrypt. It is designed specifically with password hashing in mind.

PyCrypto

The PyCrypto package is probably the most well known 3rd party cryptography package for Python. Sadly PyCrypto's development stopping in 2012. Others have continued to release the latest version of PyCryto so you can still get it for Python 3.5 if you don't mind using a 3rd party's binary. For example, I found some binary Python 3.5 wheels for PyCrypto on Github (https://github.com/sfbahr/PyCrypto-Wheels).

Fortunately there is a fork of the project called PyCrytodome that is a drop-in replacement for PyCrypto. To install it for Linux, you can use the following pip command:

```
1  pip install pycryptodome
```

Windows is a bit different:

```
1  pip install pycryptodomex
```

If you run into issues, it's probably because you don't have the right dependencies installed or you need a compiler for Windows. Check out the PyCryptodome website for additional installation help or to contact support.

Also worth noting is that PyCryptodome has many enhancements over the last version of PyCrypto. It is well worth your time to visit their home page and see what new features exist.

Encrypting a String

Once you're done checking their website out, we can move on to some examples. For our first trick, we'll use DES to encrypt a string:

```
1   >>> from Crypto.Cipher import DES
2   >>> key = b'abcdefgh'
3   >>> def pad(text):
4           while len(text) % 8 != 0:
5               text += b' '
6           return text
7   >>> des = DES.new(key, DES.MODE_ECB)
8   >>> text = b'Python rocks!'
9   >>> padded_text = pad(text)
10  >>> encrypted_text = des.encrypt(text)
11  Traceback (most recent call last):
12    File "<pyshell#35>", line 1, in <module>
13      encrypted_text = des.encrypt(text)
14    File "C:\Programs\Python\Python35-32\lib\site-packages\Crypto\Cipher\blockalgo\
15  .py", line 244, in encrypt
16      return self._cipher.encrypt(plaintext)
17  ValueError: Input strings must be a multiple of 8 in length
18  >>> encrypted_text = des.encrypt(padded_text)
19  >>> encrypted_text
20  b'>\xfc\x1f\x16x\x87\xb2\x93\x0e\xfcH\x02\xd59VQ'
```

This code is a little confusing, so let's spend some time breaking it down. First off, it should be noted that the key size for DES encryption is 8 bytes, which is why we set our key variable to a size letter string. The string that we will be encrypting must be a multiple of 8 in length, so we create a function called **pad** that can pad any string out with spaces until it's a multiple of 8. Next we create an instance of DES and some text that we want to encrypt. We also create a padded version of the text. Just for fun, we attempt to encrypt the original unpadded variant of the string which raises a **ValueError**. Here we learn that we need that padded string after all, so we pass that one in instead. As you can see, we now have an encrypted string!

Of course the example wouldn't be complete if we didn't know how to decrypt our string:

```
1   >>> des.decrypt(encrypted_text)
2   b'Python rocks!    '
```

Fortunately, that is very easy to accomplish as all we need to do is call the **decrypt** method on our des object to get our decrypted byte string back. Our next task is to learn how to encrypt and decrypt a file with PyCrypto using RSA. But first we need to create some RSA keys!

Creating an RSA key

If you want to encrypt your data with RSA, then you'll need to either have access to a public / private RSA key pair or you will need to generate your own. For this example, we will just generate our own. Since it's fairly easy to do, we will do it in Python's interpreter:

```
1  >>> from Crypto.PublicKey import RSA
2  >>> code = 'nooneknows'
3  >>> key = RSA.generate(2048)
4  >>> encrypted_key = key.exportKey(passphrase=code, pkcs=8,
5          protection="scryptAndAES128-CBC")
6  >>> with open('/path_to_private_key/my_private_rsa_key.bin', 'wb') as f:
7          f.write(encrypted_key)
8  >>> with open('/path_to_public_key/my_rsa_public.pem', 'wb') as f:
9          f.write(key.publickey().exportKey())
```

First we import **RSA** from **Crypto.PublicKey**. Then we create a silly passcode. Next we generate an RSA key of 2048 bits. Now we get to the good stuff. To generate a private key, we need to call our RSA key instance's **exportKey** method and give it our passcode, which PKCS standard to use and which encryption scheme to use to protect our private key. Then we write the file out to disk.

Next we create our public key via our RSA key instance's **publickey** method. We used a shortcut in this piece of code by just chaining the call to **exportKey** with the publickey method call to write it to disk as well.

Encrypting a File

Now that we have both a private and a public key, we can encrypt some data and write it to a file. Here's a pretty standard example:

```
1  from Crypto.PublicKey import RSA
2  from Crypto.Random import get_random_bytes
3  from Crypto.Cipher import AES, PKCS1_OAEP
4
5  with open('/path/to/encrypted_data.bin', 'wb') as out_file:
6      recipient_key = RSA.import_key(
7          open('/path_to_public_key/my_rsa_public.pem').read())
8      session_key = get_random_bytes(16)
9
10     cipher_rsa = PKCS1_OAEP.new(recipient_key)
11     out_file.write(cipher_rsa.encrypt(session_key))
12
13     cipher_aes = AES.new(session_key, AES.MODE_EAX)
14     data = b'blah blah blah Python blah blah'
15     ciphertext, tag = cipher_aes.encrypt_and_digest(data)
16
17     out_file.write(cipher_aes.nonce)
18     out_file.write(tag)
19     out_file.write(ciphertext)
```

The first three lines cover our imports from PyCryptodome. Next we open up a file to write to. Then we import our public key into a variable and create a 16-byte session key. For this example we are going to be using a hybrid encryption method, so we use PKCS#1 OAEP, which is Optimal asymmetric encryption padding. This allows us to write a data of an arbitrary length to the file. Then we create our AES cipher, create some data and encrypt the data. This will return the encrypted text and the MAC. Finally we write out the nonce, MAC (or tag) and the encrypted text.

As an aside, a nonce is an arbitrary number that is only used for crytographic communication. They are usually random or pseudorandom numbers. For AES, it must be at least 16 bytes in length. Feel free to try opening the encrypted file in your favorite text editor. You should just see gibberish.

Now let's learn how to decrypt our data:

```
1   from Crypto.PublicKey import RSA
2   from Crypto.Cipher import AES, PKCS1_OAEP
3
4   code = 'nooneknows'
5
6   with open('/path/to/encrypted_data.bin', 'rb') as fobj:
7       private_key = RSA.import_key(
8           open('/path_to_private_key/my_rsa_key.pem').read(),
9           passphrase=code)
10
11      enc_session_key, nonce, tag, ciphertext = [ fobj.read(x)
12                                            for x in (private_key.size_in_by\
13  tes(),
14                                            16, 16, -1) ]
15
16      cipher_rsa = PKCS1_OAEP.new(private_key)
17      session_key = cipher_rsa.decrypt(enc_session_key)
18
19      cipher_aes = AES.new(session_key, AES.MODE_EAX, nonce)
20      data = cipher_aes.decrypt_and_verify(ciphertext, tag)
21
22  print(data)
```

If you followed the previous example, this code should be pretty easy to parse. In this case, we are opening our encrypted file for reading in binary mode. Then we import our private key. Note that when you import the private key, you must give it your passcode. Otherwise you will get an error. Next we read in our file. You will note that we read in the private key first, then the next 16 bytes for the nonce, which is followed by the next 16 bytes which is the tag and finally the rest of the file, which is our data.

Then we need to decrypt our session key, recreate our AES key and decrypt the data.

You can use PyCryptodome to do much, much more. However we need to move on and see what else we can use for our cryptographic needs in Python.

The cryptography Package

The **cryptography** package aims to be "cryptography for humans" much like the **requests** library is "HTTP for Humans". The idea is that you will be able to create simple cryptographic recipes that are safe and easy-to-use. If you need to, you can drop down to low=level cryptographic primitives, which require you to know what you're doing or you might end up creating something that's not very secure.

If you are using Python 3.5, you can install it with pip, like so:

```
1  pip install cryptography
```

You will see that cryptography installs a few dependencies along with itself. Assuming that they all completed successfully, we can try encrypting some text. Let's give the **Fernet** module a try. The Fernet module implements an easy-to-use authentication scheme that uses a symmetric encryption algorithm which guarantees that any message you encrypt with it cannot be manipulated or read without the key you define. The Fernet module also supports key rotation via **MultiFernet**. Let's take a look at a simple example:

```
1  >>> from cryptography.fernet import Fernet
2  >>> cipher_key = Fernet.generate_key()
3  >>> cipher_key
4  b'APM1JDVgT8WDGOWBgQv6EIhvxl4vDYvUnVdg-Vjdt0o='
5  >>> cipher = Fernet(cipher_key)
6  >>> text = b'My super secret message'
7  >>> encrypted_text = cipher.encrypt(text)
8  >>> encrypted_text
9  (b'gAAAAABXOnV86aeUGADA6mTe9xEL92y_m0_TlC9vcqaF6NzHqRKkjEqh4d21PInEP3C9HuiUkS9f'
10  b'6bdHsS1RiCNWbSkPuRd_62zfEv3eaZjJvLAm3omnya8=')
11  >>> decrypted_text = cipher.decrypt(encrypted_text)
12  >>> decrypted_text
13  b'My super secret message'
```

First off we need to import Fernet. Next we generate a key. We print out the key to see what it looks like. As you can see, it's a random byte string. If you want, you can try running the **generate_key** method a few times. The result will always be different. Next we create our Fernet cipher instance using our key.

Now we have a cipher we can use to encrypt and decrypt our message. The next step is to create a message worth encrypting and then encrypt it using the **encrypt** method. I went ahead and printed our the encrypted text so you can see that you can no longer read the text. To decrypt our super secret message, we just call **decrypt** on our cipher and pass it the encrypted text. The result is we get a plain text byte string of our message.

Wrapping Up

This chapter barely scratched the surface of what you can do with PyCryptodome and the cryptography packages. However it does give you a decent overview of what can be done with Python in regards to encrypting and decrypting strings and files. Be sure to read the documentation and start experimenting to see what else you can do!

Chapter 15 - Databases

This chapter is about how you connect to and work with databases in Python. It is a general purpose chapter. You will not learn the complete SQL language in one chapter. Instead, I will give you high level overview of some SQL commands and then we will look at how to connect to some of the most popular databases with Python. Most databases use the basic SQL commands in the same way, but they also may have some commands that are specific for that database backend or that just work slightly differently. Be sure to read your database documentation should you run into issues.

We will start the chapter by learning some very basic SQL syntax.

Basic SQL Syntax

SQL stands for Structured Query Language. It is basically the defacto language for interacting with databases and is a primitive computer programming language in its own right. In this section, we will learn how the basics of CRUD, which stands for Create, Read, Update and Delete. These are the most important functions you need to get started using a database. Of course, you will also need to know how to query, but we'll cover that as we go along as you will need to query in order to read, update or delete.

Creating a Table

The first thing you need in a database is a table. This is where you data will be stored and organized. Most of the time, you will have multiple tables where each table holds a sub-set of your data. Creating a table in SQL is easy. All you need to do is something like this:

```
1   CREATE TABLE table_name (
2       id INTEGER,
3       name VARCHAR,
4       make VARCHAR
5       model VARCHAR,
6       year DATE,
7       PRIMARY KEY (id)
8       );
```

This is pretty generic, but it works in most cases. The first item of note is that we have a bunch of capitalized words. These are the SQL commands. They don't usually need to be in caps, but we're doing that here to help you see them. I want to also note that each database supports slightly different commands. Most will have a CREATE TABLE, but the database column types might be different. You will note that in this example, we have INTEGER, VARCHAR and DATE data types. DATE can be called a lot of different things and VARCHAR can as well. Consult your documentation for what you will need to do.

Regardless, what we're doing in this example is creating a database with five columns. The first one is an **id** that we set as our primary key. It should not be NULL, but we don't specify that here as once again, each database backend does that differently or does it automatically for us. The other columns should be pretty self explanatory.

Inserting Data

Right now our database is empty. That's not very useful, so in this section we will learn how to add some data to it. Here's the general idea:

```
1   INSERT INTO table_name (id, name, make, model, year)
2   VALUES (1, 'Marly', 'Ford', 'Explorer', '2000');
```

SQL uses the INSERT INTO commands to add data to the specified database. You also specify why columns you are adding data too. When we create the table, we can specify required column which could cause an error to be raised if we didn't add data to a required column. However we didn't do that in our table definition earlier. It's just something to keep in mind. You will also receive an error if you pass the wrong data type, which I did for the year. I passed in a string or varchar instead of a date. Of course, each database requires a different date format, so you'll want to figure out what DATE even means for your database.

Updating Data

Let's say we made a typo in our previous INSERT. To fix that, we need to use SQL's UPDATE command:

```
1  UPDATE table_name
2  SET name='Chevrolet'
3  WHERE id=1;
```

The UPDATE command tells us which table we are going to update. Next we SET one or more columns to a new value. Finally we need to tell the database which row we want to update. We can use the WHERE command to tell the database we want to change the row that has an id of 1.

Reading Data

Reading data from our database is done via SQL's SELECT statement:

```
1  SELECT name, make, model
2  FROM table_name;
```

This will return all the rows from the database but the result will only contain three pieces of data: the name, make and model. If you want to grab all the data in the database, you can do this:

```
1  SELECT * FROM table_name;
```

The asterisk is a wildcard that tells SQL you want to grab all the columns. If you want to limit the scope of your select, you can add a WHERE to your query:

```
1  SELECT name, make, model
2  FROM table_name
3  WHERE year >= '2000-01-01' AND
4       year <= '2006-01-01';
```

This will get back the name, make and model information for the years 2000 - 2006. There are a lot of other SQL commands to help you in your queries. Be sure to check out BETWEEN, LIKE, ORDER BY, DISTINCT and JOIN.

Deleting Data

Occasionally you will need to delete data from your database. Here's how:

```
1  DELETE FROM table_name
2  WHERE name='Ford';
```

This will delete all rows that have the name field set to 'Ford' from our table. If you wanted to delete the entire table, you would use the DROP statement:

```
1  DROP TABLE table_name;
```

Be careful when using DROP and DELETE as you can easily lose most or all of your data if you call the statement incorrectly. Always make sure you have a good, tested backup of your database.

adodbapi

Back in Python 2.4 and 2.5 days, I needed to connect to SQL Server 2005 and Microsoft Access and one or both were set up to only use Microsoft's ADO connection methodology. The solution at that time was to use the **adodbapi** package. This package should be used when you need to access a database via Microsoft ADO. I should also note that this package hasn't been updated since 2014, so keep that in mind as well. Hopefully you won't need to use this package as Microsoft also provides an ODBC connection driver nowadays, but should you have to support ADO-only for some reason, then this is the package for you!

Note: adodbapi depends on having the PyWin32 package installed.

To install adodbapi, you just need to do the following:

```
1  pip install adodbapi
```

Let's take a look at a simple example I used to connect to Microsoft Access long ago:

```
1  import adodbapi
2
3  database = "db1.mdb"
4  constr = 'Provider=Microsoft.Jet.OLEDB.4.0; Data Source=%s' % database
5  tablename = "address"
6
7  # connect to the database
8  conn = adodbapi.connect(constr)
9
10 # create a cursor
11 cur = conn.cursor()
12
13 # extract all the data
14 sql = "select * from %s" % tablename
15 cur.execute(sql)
16
17 # show the result
18 result = cur.fetchall()
19 for item in result:
```

```
20       print item
21
22   # close the cursor and connection
23   cur.close()
24   conn.close()
```

First we create a connection string. These strings specify how to connect to Microsoft Access or SQL Server. In this case, we are connecting to Access. To actually connect to the database, you call the **connect** method and pass it your connection string. Now you have a connection object but to interact with the database, you will need a **cursor**. We create that next. The next piece is to actually write a SQL query. In this case, we want everything in the database, so we select * and then pass that SQL statement to our cursor's **execute** method. To get the result, we call **fetchall**, which will return all the results. Finally we close the cursor and then the connection.

If you do end up using the adodbapi package, I highly recommend looking up their quick reference document. It is very helpful in figuring out the package as it isn't documented all that well.

pyodbc

Open Database Connectivity (ODBC) is a standard API for accessing databases. Most production databases have an ODBC driver available that you can install to access their database with.

One of the most popular methods of connecting via ODBC with Python is the pyodbc package. According to its page on the Python Packaging Index, you can use it on Windows or Linux. The pyodbc package implements the DB API 2.0 specification. You can install pyodbc with pip:

```
1   pip install pyodbc
```

Let's look at a fairly generic way to connect to SQL Server with pyodbc and select some data like we did in the adodbapi section:

```
1   import pyodbc
2
3   driver = 'DRIVER={SQL Server}'
4   server = 'SERVER=localhost'
5   port = 'PORT=1433'
6   db = 'DATABASE=testdb'
7   user = 'UID=me'
8   pw = 'PWD=pass'
9   conn_str = ';'.join([driver, server, port, db, user, pw])
10
11  conn = pyodbc.connect(conn_str)
```

```
12  cursor = conn.cursor()
13
14  cursor.execute('select * from table_name')
15  row = cursor.fetchone()
16  rest_of_rows = cursor.fetchall()
```

In this code, we create a very long connection string. It has many parts. The driver, server port number, database name, user and password. You would probably want to save most of this information into some kind of configuration file so you wouldn't have to enter it each time. The username and password should never be hard coded, although you will find that it happens from time to time in the real world.

Once we have our connection string, we attempt to connect to the database via the **connection** function call. If it connects successfully, then we now have a connection object which we can use to create a cursor object from. Now that we have a cursor, we can query the database and run any other commands that we need to depending on what our database permissions are. In this example, we run a SELECT * on our database to extract all rows. Then we demonstrate that you can just grab one row at a time or pull them all via **fetchone** and **fetchall** respectively. There is also a **fetchmany** function that you can use to specify how many rows you want returned.

If you have a database that works with ODBC, you should give this package a try. Note that Microsoft databases are not the only databases that support this connection method.

pypyodbc

The **pypyodbc** package is actually just one pure Python script. It is basically a reimplementation of pyodbc but in pure Python. What this means is that pyodbc is a Python wrapper around a C++ backend whereas pypyodbc is only Python code. It supports the same API as the previous module so you should be able to use them interchangeably in most cases. Thus I won't be showing any examples here since the only difference is the import.

MySQL

MySQL is a very popular open source database backend. You can connect to it with Python in several different ways. For example, you could connect to it using one of the ODBC methods I mentioned in the last two sections. One of the most popular ways to connect to MySQL with Python is the MySQLdb package. There are actually a couple of variants of this package:

- MySQLdb1
- MySQLdb2
- moist

The first is the traditional way to connect to MySQL with Python. However it is basically only in maintenance only development now and won't be receiving any new features. The developers switched to doing MySQLdb2 and then transformed that into the **moist** project. MySQL had a rift occur after they were bought by Oracle and it ended up getting forked into a project called Maria. So now there is Maria, MySQL and another fork called Drizzle that are all based on some portion of the original MySQL code. The **moist** project attempts to create a bridge we can use to connect to all three of these backends, although it's still a bit in the alpha or beta stages at the time of publication. To make things extra confusing, MySQLdb is a wrapper around **_mysql**, which you can use directly if you want to.

After all of that, you'll quickly learn that MySQLdb is not compatible with Python 3 at all. The moist project will be some day, but it's not there yet. So what does one use with Python 3? You have a few choices:

- mysql-connector-python
- pymysql
- CyMySQL
- mysqlclient

The **mysqlclient** is a fork of MySQL-python (i.e. MySQLdb) that adds Python 3 support. It is also the method that the Django project recommends for connecting to MySQL. So we will focus our time looking at this package in this section.

Note that you will need to have MySQL or a MySQL Client installed before you can successfully install the **mysqlclient** package. But if you have those prerequisites, then you can just use pip to get it installed:

```
1  pip install mysqlclient
```

Let's look at a quick example of its usage:

```
1  import MySQLdb
2
3  conn = MySQLdb.connect('localhost', 'username', 'password', 'table_name')
4  cursor = conn.cursor()
5
6  cursor.execute("SELECT * FROM table_name")
7
8  # get a single row
9  row = cursor.fetchone()
10 print(row)
11
12 # disconnect from the database
13 conn.close()
```

This code probably looks pretty familiar to you. Most good database related packages follow the same API. So in this one, we import our package and create a connection. You will note that we need to know the name of the server we're connecting too (localhost, an IP, etc), the username and password to connect with and the table that we want to interact with.

Next we create a cursor object so we can execute SQL commands which we do in the very next line of code. Finally we fetch one row from the result, print it out and close our database connection.

I want to stop here and note that the documentation for this is pretty lousy. There really isn't much for official documentation other than the code so you will need to rely on that and the few tutorials that are out there.

PostgreSQL

PostgreSQL is another popular open source database that a lot o people like to use. Python has quite a few different packages that support this backend, but the most popular is **Psycopg**. The Psycopg package supports Python 2.5-2.7 and Python 3.1-3.4. It will likely work with Python 3.5 too if you build it yourself.

Unfortunately, Psycopg doesn't support pip for installation, so you will need to consult their documentation on how to get it installed. The reason is that each operating system has a different installation method.

Once it is installed, you can try out the following code:

```python
import psycopg2

conn = psycopg2.connect(dbname='my_database', user='username')
cursor = conn.cursor()

# execute a query
cursor.execute("SELECT * FROM table_name")
row = cursor.fetchone()

# close your cursor and connection
cursor.close()
conn.close()
```

As expected, the Psycopg package follows the standard API that we've been seeing. Here we just import the package and connect to our database. Then we create our cursor and run our lovely SELECT * statement. Finally we grab the first row of data from the result via **fetchone**. Finally we close down our cursor and connection.

Object Relational Mappers

If you do a lot of database work, you might want to consider checking out an Object Relational Mapper (ORM). An Object Relational Mapper allows you to work with the database without using SQL itself. Some developers call it more "Pythonic" since it's not a mix of Python code and SQL. The most popular ORM in Python is SQLAlchemy.

One of the major benefits to using SQLAlchemy is that you can usually write your database code once and then if the backend changes you won't have to change any of your queries. The only thing you would need to change is he connection string. I have used SQLAlchemy to transfer a tables from one backend to another and been able to use the same code for both ends.

There are other ORMs such as SQLObject and peewee. When I first started out, I tried SQLObject, but it didn't support composite keys at that time, so I had to switch to SQLAlchemy. I never regretted it though. The peewee package is a small, lightweight ORM, but it also isn't as flexible as SQLAlchemy is.

I highly recommend reading up on the various implementations and see which one works the best for you.

Wrapping Up

This chapter covered a lot of different topics. You learned the barebones basics of SQL. Then you learned about some of the different ways you can connect to databases using Python. This was not an exhaustive list by any means though. There are many other packages you can use to connect to thse databases and others too. For example, we didn't even learn about connecting to MongoDb or other NoSQL databases even though they are well supported by Python too.

If the database is even moderately popular then there's probably a way to hook into it with Python. You should spend some time checking out some of these packages for yourself. Have fun!

Chapter 16 - The super built-in

The **super** built-in function was introduced way back in Python 2.2. The super function will return a proxy object that will delegate method calls to a parent or sibling class of type. If that was a little unclear, what it allows you to do is access inherited methods that have been overridden in a class. The super function has two use cases. The first is in single inheritance where super can be used to refer to the parent class or classes without actually naming them explicitly. This can make your code more maintainable in the future. This is similar to the behavior that you will find in other programming languages, like Dylan's *next-method*.

The second use case is in a dynamic execution environment where super supports cooperative multiple inheritance. This is actually a pretty unique use case that may only apply to Python as it is not found in languages that only support single inheritance nor in statically compiled languages.

super has had its fair share of controversy even among core developers. The original documentation was confusing and using super was tricky. There were some who even labeled super as harmful, although that article seems to apply more to the Python 2 implementation of super then the Python 3 version. We will start out this chapter by looking at how to call super in both Python 2 and 3. Then we will learn about **Method Resolution Order**.

Python 2 vs Python 3

Let's start by looking at a regular class definition. Then we'll add super using Python 2 to see how it changes.

```
1  class MyParentClass(object):
2      def __init__(self):
3          pass
4
5  class SubClass(MyParentClass):
6      def __init__(self):
7          MyParentClass.__init__(self)
```

This is a pretty standard set up for single inheritance. We have a base class and then the subclass. Another name for base class is parent class or even super class. Anyway, in the subclass we need to initialize the parent class too. The core developers of Python thought it would be a good idea to make this kind of thing more abstract and portable, so the super function was added. In Python 2, the subclass would look like this:

```
1  class SubClass(MyParentClass):
2      def __init__(self):
3          super(SubClass, self).__init__()
```

Python 3 simplified this a bit. Let's take a look:

```
1  class MyParentClass():
2      def __init__(self):
3          pass
4
5  class SubClass(MyParentClass):
6      def __init__(self):
7          super().__init__()
```

The first change you will notice is that the parent class no longer needs to be explicitly based on the **object** base class. The second change is the call to **super**. We no longer need to pass it anything and yet super does the right thing implicitly. Most classes actually have arguments passed to them though, so let's look at how the super signature changes in that case:

```
1  class MyParentClass():
2      def __init__(self, x, y):
3          pass
4
5  class SubClass(MyParentClass):
6      def __init__(self, x, y):
7          super().__init__(x, y)
```

Here we just need to call the super's **__init__** method and pass the arguments along. It's still nice and straight-forward.

Method Resolution Order (MRO)

Method Resolution Order (MRO) is just a list of types that the class is derived from. So if you have a class that inherits from two other classes, you might think that it's MRO will be itself and the two parents it inherits from. However the parents also inherit from Python's base class: **object**. Let's take a look at an example that will make this clearer:

```
1   class X:
2       def __init__(self):
3           print('X')
4           super().__init__()
5
6   class Y:
7       def __init__(self):
8           print('Y')
9           super().__init__()
10
11  class Z(X, Y):
12      pass
13
14
15  z = Z()
16  print(Z.__mro__)
```

Here we create 3 classes. The first two just print out the name of the class and the last one inherits from the previous two. Then we instantiate the class and also print out its MRO:

```
1   X
2   Y
3   (<class '__main__.Z'>, <class '__main__.X'>, <class '__main__.Y'>, <class 'objec\
4   t'>)
```

As you can see, when you instantiate it, each of the parent classes prints out its name. Then we get the Method Resolution Order, which is ZXY and object. Another good example to look at is to see what happens when you create a class variable in the base class and then override it later:

```
1   class Base:
2       var = 5
3       def __init__(self):
4           pass
5
6   class X(Base):
7       def __init__(self):
8           print('X')
9           super().__init__()
10
11  class Y(Base):
12      var = 10
13      def __init__(self):
```

```
14              print('Y')
15              super().__init__()
16
17   class Z(X, Y):
18       pass
19
20
21   z = Z()
22   print(Z.__mro__)
23   print(super(Z, z).var)
```

So in this example, we create a Base class with a class variable set to 5. Then we create subclasses of our Base class: X and Y. Y overrides the Base class's class variable and sets it to 10. Finally we create class Z which inherits from X and Y. When we call super on class Z, which class variable will get printed? Try running this code and you'll get the following result:

```
1   X
2   Y
3   (<class '__main__.Z'>, <class '__main__.X'>, <class '__main__.Y'>, <class '__mai\
4   n__.Base'>, <class 'object'>)
5   10
```

Let's parse this out a bit. Class Z inherits from X and Y. So when we ask it what it's **var** is, the MRO will look at X to see if it is defined. It's not there, so it moves on to Y. Y has it, so that is what gets returned. Try adding a class variable to X and you will see that it overrides Y because it is first in the Method Resolution Order.

There is a wonderful document that a fellow named Michele Simionato created that describes Python's Method Resolution Order in detail. You can check it out here: https://www.python.org/download/releases/2.3/mro/. It's a long read and you'll probably need to re-read portions of it a few times, but it explains MRO very well. By the way, you might note that this article is labeled as being for Python 2.3, but it still applies even in Python 3, even though the calling of super is a bit different now.

The super method was updated slightly in Python 3. In Python 3, super can figure out what class it is invoked from as well as the first argument of the containing method. It will even work when the first argument is not called **self**! This is what you see when you call **super()** in Python 3. In Python 2, you would need to call **super(ClassName, self)**, but that is simplified in Python 3.

Because of this fact, super knows how to interpret the MRO and it stores this information in the following magic propertie: **__thisclass__** and **__self_class__**. Let's look at an example:

```
1   class Base():
2       def __init__(self):
3           s = super()
4           print(s.__thisclass__)
5           print(s.__self_class__)
6           s.__init__()
7
8   class SubClass(Base):
9       pass
10
11  sub = SubClass()
```

Here we create a base class and assign the super call to a variable so we can find out what those magic properties contain. Then we print them out and initialize. Finally we create a SubClass of the Base class and instantiate the SubClass. The result that gets printed to stdout is this:

```
1   <class '__main__.Base'>
2   <class '__main__.SubClass'>
```

This is pretty cool, but probably not all that handy unless you're doing a metaclasses or mixin classes.

Wrapping Up

There are lots of interesting examples of super that you will see on the internet. Most of them tend to be a bit mind-bending at first, but then you'll figure them out and either think it's really cool or wonder why you'd do that. Personally I haven't had a need for super in most of my work, but it can be useful for forward compatibility. What this means is that you want your code to work in the future with as few changes as possible. So you might start off with single inheritance today, but a year or two down the road, you might add another base class. If you use super correctly, then this will be a lot easier to add. I have also seen arguments for using super for dependency injection, but I haven't seen any good, concrete examples of this latter use case. It's a good thing to keep in mind though.

The super function can be very handy or it can be really confusing or a little bit of both. Use it wisely and it will serve you well.

Chapter 17 - Descriptors

Descriptors were introduced to Python way back in version 2.2. They provide the developer with the ability to add managed attributes to objects. The methods needed to create a descriptor are __get__, __set__ and __delete__. If you define any of these methods, then you have created a descriptor.

The idea behind the descriptor is to get, set or delete attributes from your object's dictionary. When you access a class attribute, this starts the lookup chain. Should the looked up value be an object with one of our descriptor methods defined, then the descriptor method will be invoked.

Descriptors power a lot of the magic of Python's internals. They are what make properties, methods and even the **super** function work. They are also used to implement the new style classes that were also introduced in Python 2.2.

The Descriptor Protocol

The protocol to create a descriptor is really quite easy. You only need to define one or more of the following:

- __get__(self, obj, type=None), returns value
- __set__(self, obj, value), returns None
- __delete__(self, obj), returns None

Once you've defined at least one, you have created a descriptor. If you can you define both __get__ and __set__, you will have created a data descriptor. A descriptor with only __get__() defined are known as non-data descriptors and are usually used for methods. The reason for this distinction in descriptor types is that if an instance's dictionary happens to have a data descriptor, the descriptor will take precedence during the lookup. If the instance's dictionary has an entry that matches up with a non-data descriptor, then the dictionary's own entry will take precedence over the descriptor.

You can also create a read-only descriptor if you define both __get__ and __set__, but raise an **AttributeError** when the __set__ method is called.

Calling a Descriptor

The most common method of calling a descriptor is for the descriptor to be invoked automatically when you access an attribute. A typical example would be `my_obj.attribute_name`. This will cause your object to look up `attribute_name` in the `my_obj` object. If your `attribute_name` happens to define `__get__()`, then `attribute_name.__get__(my_obj)` will get called. This all depends on whether your instance is an object or a class.

The magic behind this lies in the magic method known as __getattribute__, which will turn `my_-obj.a` into this: `type(my_obj).__dict__['a'].__get__(a, type(a))`. You can read all about the implementation in Python's documentation here: https://docs.python.org/3/howto/descriptor.html.

According to said documentation, there are a few points to keep in mind in regards to calling a descriptor:

- The descriptor is invoked via the default implementation of the __getattribute__-method
- If you override __getattribute__, this will prevent the descriptor from getting automatically called
- object.__getattribute__() and type.__getattribute__() don't call __get__() the same way
- A data descriptor will always, ALWAYS override instance dictionaries
- The non-data descriptor can be overridden by instance dictionaries.

More information on how all this works can be found in Python's data model (https://docs.python.org/3/reference/datamodel.html#object.__getattribute__), the Python source code and in Guido van Rossum's document, "Unifying types and class in Python", which can be found here: https://www.python.org/download/releases/2.2.3/descrintro/#cooperation

Descriptor Examples

At this point, you may be confused how you would even use a descriptor. I always find it helpful when I am learning a new concept if I have a few examples that demonstrate how it works. So in this section, we will look at some examples so you will know how to use descriptors in your own code!

Let's start by writing a really simple data descriptor and then use it in a class. This example is based on one from Python's documentation:

```
1   class MyDescriptor():
2       """
3       A simple demo descriptor
4       """
5       def __init__(self, initial_value=None, name='my_var'):
6           self.var_name = name
7           self.value = initial_value
8
9       def __get__(self, obj, objtype):
10          print('Getting', self.var_name)
11          return self.value
12
13      def __set__(self, obj, value):
14          msg = 'Setting {name} to {value}'
15          print(msg.format(name=self.var_name, value=value))
16          self.value = value
17
18  class MyClass():
19      desc = MyDescriptor(initial_value='Mike', name='desc')
20      normal = 10
21
22  if __name__ == '__main__':
23      c = MyClass()
24      print(c.desc)
25      print(c.normal)
26      c.desc = 100
27      print(c.desc)
```

Here we create a class and define three magic methods:

- __init__ - our constructor which takes a value and the name of our variable
- __get__ - prints out the current variable name and returns the value
- __set__ - prints out the name of our variable and the value we just assigned and sets the value itself

Then we create a class that creates an instance of our descriptor as a class attribute and also creates a normal class attribute. Then we run a few "tests" by creating an instance of our normal class and accessing our class attributes. Here is the output:

```
1   Getting desc
2   Mike
3   10
4   Setting desc to 100
5   Getting desc
6   100
```

As you can see, when we access **c.desc**, it prints out our "Getting" message and we print out what it returns, which is "Mike". Next we print out the regular class attribute's value. Finally we change the descriptor variable's value, which causes our "Setting" message to be printed. We also double-check the current value to make sure that it was actually set, which is why you see that last "Getting" message.

Python uses descriptors underneath the covers to build properties, bound / unbound methods and class methods. If you look up the property class in Python's documentation, you will see that it follows the descriptor protocol very closely:

property(fget=None, fset=None, fdel=None, doc=None)

It clearly shows that the property class has a getter, setter and a deleting method.

Let's look at another example where we use a descriptor to do validation:

```
1   from weakref import WeakKeyDictionary
2
3   class Drinker:
4       def __init__(self):
5           self.req_age = 21
6           self.age = WeakKeyDictionary()
7
8       def __get__(self, instance_obj, objtype):
9           return self.age.get(instance_obj, self.req_age)
10
11      def __set__(self, instance, new_age):
12          if new_age < 21:
13              msg = '{name} is too young to legally imbibe'
14              raise Exception(msg.format(name=instance.name))
15          self.age[instance] = new_age
16          print('{name} can legally drink in the USA'.format(
17              name=instance.name))
18
19      def __delete__(self, instance):
20          del self.age[instance]
```

```
21
22
23   class Person:
24       drinker_age = Drinker()
25
26       def __init__(self, name, age):
27           self.name = name
28           self.drinker_age = age
29
30
31   p = Person('Miguel', 30)
32   p = Person('Niki', 13)
```

Once again, we create a descriptor class. In this case, we use Python's **weakref** library's **WeakKey-Dictionary**, which is a neat class that creates a dictionary that maps keys weakly. What this means is that when there are no strong references to a key in the dictionary, that key and its value will be discarded. We are using that in this example to prevent our Person instances from hanging around indefinitely.

Anyway, the part of the descriptor that we care most about is in our __set__ method. Here we check to see that the instance's **age** parameter is greater than 21, which is what you would need to be in the USA if you wanted to drink an alcoholic beverage. If you're age is lower, then it will raise an exception. Otherwise it will print out the name of the person and a message. To test out our descriptor, we create two instances with one that is greater than 21 in age and one that is less. If you run this code you should see the following output:

```
1   Miguel can legally drink in the USA
2   Traceback (most recent call last):
3     File "desc_validator.py", line 32, in <module>
4       p = Person('Niki', 13)
5     File "desc_validator.py", line 28, in __init__
6       self.drinker_age = age
7     File "desc_validator.py", line 14, in __set__
8       raise Exception(msg.format(name=instance.name))
9   Exception: Niki is too young to legally imbibe
```

That obviously worked the way it was supposed to, but it's not really obvious how it worked. The reason this works the way it does is that when we go to set **drinker_age**, Python notices that it is a descriptor. Python knows that **drinker_age** is a descriptor because we defined it as such when we created it as a class attribute:

```
1   drinker_age = Drinker()
```

So when we go to set it, we actually call our descriptor's __set__ method which passes in the instance and the age that we are trying to set. If the age is less than 21, then we raise an exception with a custom message. Otherwise we print out a message that you are old enough.

Getting back to how this all works, if we were to try to print out the drinker_age, Python would execute Person.drinker_age.__get__. Since drinker_age is a descriptor, its __get__ is what actually gets called. If you wanted to set the drinker_age, you would do this:

```
1   p.drinker_age = 32
```

Python would then call **Person.drinker_age.__set__** and since that method is also implemented in our descriptor, then the descriptor method is the one that gets called. Once you trace your way through the code execution a few times, you will quickly see how this all works.

The main thing to remember is that descriptors are linked to classes and not to instances.

Wrapping Up

Descriptors are pretty important because of all the places they are used in Python's source code. They can be really useful to you too if you understand how they work. However, their use cases are pretty limited and you probably won't be using them very often. Hopefully this chapter will have helped you see the descriptor's usefulness and when you might want to use one yourself.

Chapter 18 - Scope

You will hear the term **scope** mentioned in most beginning computer science classes. It's a pretty important topic that can cause some pretty confusing errors if you don't understand how it works. A scope basically tells the interpreter when a name (or variable) is visible. In other words, the scope defines when and where you can use your variables, functions, etc. When you try to use something that isn't in your current scope, you will usually get a **NameError**.

Python has three different types of scope:

- local scope
- global scope
- nonlocal scope (which was added in Python 3)

Let's learn how each of these scopes work.

Local Scope

Local scope is the scope you will use the most in Python. When you create a variable in a code block, it will be resolved using the nearest enclosing scope or scopes. The grouping of all these scopes is known as the code blocks *environment*. In other words, all assignments are done in local scope by default. If you want something different, then you'll need to set your variable to **global** or **nonlocal**, which we will be looking at later on in this chapter.

For now, we will create a simple example using Python's interpreter that demonstrates local scope assignment!

```
1  >>> x = 10
2  >>> def my_func(a, b):
3          print(x)
4          print(z)
5
6
7  >>> my_func(1, 2)
8  10
9  Traceback (most recent call last):
10   File "<pyshell#19>", line 1, in <module>
11     my_func(1, 2)
12   File "<pyshell#18>", line 3, in my_func
13     print(z)
14 NameError: name 'z' is not defined
```

Here we create variable x and a very simple function that takes two arguments. It then prints x and z. Note that we haven't defined z so when we call the function, we receive a NameError. This happens because z is not defined or is outside the scope. If you define z before you call the function, then z will be found and you won't receive the NameError.

You will also receive a NameError if you try to access a variable that is inside the function only:

```
1  def my_func(a, b):
2      i = 2
3      print(x)
4
5  if __name__ == '__main__':
6      x = 10
7      my_func(1, 2)
8      print(i)
```

The variable, i, is only defined inside the function, so when you run this code you will get a NameError.

Let's modify the first example a bit. Put the following into a file and try running it:

```
1  def my_func(a, b):
2      x = 5
3      print(x)
4
5  if __name__ == '__main__':
6      x = 10
7      my_func(1, 2)
8      print(x)
```

What do you think will happen? Will it print 10 twice? No, it will not. The reason is that we now have two x variables. The x inside of **my_func** has a local function scope and overrides the x variable outside of the function. So when we call my_func, we get 5 printed out instead of 10. Then when the function returns, the x variable inside of my_func is garbage collected and the scope for the outer x comes back into play. This is why the last print statement prints out a 10.

If you want to get really tricky, you can try printing x before we assign it in our function:

```
1  def my_func(a, b):
2      print(x)
3      x = 5
4      print(x)
5
6  if __name__ == '__main__':
7      x = 10
8      my_func(1, 2)
9      print(x)
```

When you run this code, you will receive an exception:

```
1  UnboundLocalError: local variable 'x' referenced before assignment
```

This occurs because Python notices that you are assigning x later on in **my_func** and thus it raises an error because x hasn't been defined yet.

Global Scope

Python includes the **global** statement. It is a keyword of Python. The global statement declares a variable as being available for the code block following the statement. While you can create a name before you declare it global, this is strongly discouraged. Let's attempt to use global to fix our exception from the last example:

```
1  def my_func(a, b):
2      global x
3      print(x)
4      x = 5
5      print(x)
6
7  if __name__ == '__main__':
8      x = 10
9      my_func(1, 2)
10     print(x)
```

The output for this code will be this:

```
1  10
2  5
3  5
```

By declaring x to be a global, we tell Python to use the first declaration of x for our first print statement in the function. Then we give x a new value, 5, and print it again before exiting our function. You will notice that since x is now global when we reach the last print statement at the end of the code, x is still 5.

Let's make things extra interesting by mixing globals and locals:

```
1  def my_func(a, b):
2      global c
3      # swap a and b
4      b, a = a, b
5      d = 'Mike'
6      print(a, b, c, d)
7
8  a, b, c, d = 1, 2, 'c is global', 4
9  my_func(1, 2)
10 print(a, b, c, d)
```

Here we set variable *c* as global. This should make c print out the same both inside and outside our function. We also swap the values of variables a and b in the function to show that we can reassign them inside the function without modifying them outside. This demonstrates that the a and b variables are not global. If you run this code, you should see the following output:

```
1  2 1 c is global Mike
2  1 2 c is global 4
```

I just want to note that you shouldn't modify global variables inside of a function. This is considered bad practice by the Python community and it can make debugging quite a bit harder as well.

Now that we understand locals and globals we can move on to learn about **non_local** scope.

nonlocal Scope

Python 3 added a new keyword called **nonlocal**. The nonlocal keyword adds a scope override to the inner scope. You can read all about it in PEP 3104. This is best illustrated with a couple of code examples. One of the most common examples is to create function that can increment:

```
1  def counter():
2      num = 0
3      def incrementer():
4          num += 1
5          return num
6      return incrementer
```

If you try running this code, you will receive an **UnboundLocalError** because the **num** variable is referenced before it is assigned in the innermost function. Let's add nonlocal to the mix:

```
1  >>> def counter():
2          num = 0
3          def incrementer():
4              nonlocal num
5              num += 1
6              return num
7          return incrementer
8  >>> c = counter()
9  >>> c
10 <function counter.<locals>.incrementer at 0x7f45caf44048>
11 >>> c()
12 1
13 >>> c()
14 2
15 >>> c()
16 3
```

Now our incrementing function works as we expected it to. As a side note, this type of function is known as a **closure**. A closure is basically a block of code that "closes" nonlocal variables. The idea behind a closure is that you can reference variables that are defined outside of your function.

Basically nonlocal will allow you to assign to variables in an outer scope, but not a global scope. So you can't use nonlocal in our **counter** function because then it would try to assign to a global scope. Give it a try and you will quickly get a **SyntaxError**. Instead you must use nonlocal in a nested function.

Wrapping Up

In this chapter, we learned that we can change how a variable is referenced using Python global and nonlocal keywords. We learned where you can use and why you might want to. We also learned about local scope. Have fun and keep experimenting!

Part III - Working with the Web

The Internet or World Wide Web is a vast series of websites that is ever changing and ever growing. This section of the book will look at some of the ways that we can use the Python programming language to interact with websites. Specifically, we will be covering the following:

- Chapter 19 - Web scraping
- Chapter 20 - Working with web APIs
- Chapter 21 - Python's ftplib
- Chapter 22 - Python's urllib

These topics will be useful to you for interacting with the websites that you encounter. You will also learn how to extract data from websites to use for your own purposes.

Let's get started!

Chapter 19 - Web Scraping

Web scraping is where a programmer will write an application to download web pages and parse out specific information from them. Usually when you are scraping data you will need to make your application navigate the website programmatically. In this chapter, we will learn how to download files from the internet and parse them if need be. We will also learn how to create a simple spider that we can use to crawl a website.

Tips for Scraping

There are a few tips that we need to go over before we start scraping.

- Always check the website's terms and conditions **before** you scrape them. They usually have terms that limit how often you can scrape or what you can you scrape
- Because your script will run much faster than a human can browse, make sure you don't hammer their website with lots of requests. This may even be covered in the terms and conditions of the website.
- You can get into legal trouble if you overload a website with your requests or you attempt to use it in a way that violates the terms and conditions you agreed to.
- Websites change all the time, so your scraper will break some day. Know this: You will have to maintain your scraper if you want it to keep working.
- Unfortunately the data you get from websites can be a mess. As with any data parsing activity, you will need to clean it up to make it useful to you.

With that out of the way, let's start scraping!

Preparing to Scrape

Before we can start scraping, we need to figure out what we want to do. We will be using my blog for this example. Our task will be to scrape the titles and links to the articles on the front page of my blog, which can be found here: http://www.blog.pythonlibrary.org/. You can use Python's **urllib2** module to download the HTML that we need to parse or you can use the **requests** library. For this example, I'll be using requests.

Most websites nowadays have pretty complex HTML. Fortunately most browsers provide tools to make figuring out where website elements are quite trivial. For example, if you open my blog in chrome, you can right click on any of the article titles and click the **Inspect** menu option (see below):

Once you've clicked that, you will see a sidebar appear that highlights the tag that contains the title. It looks like this:

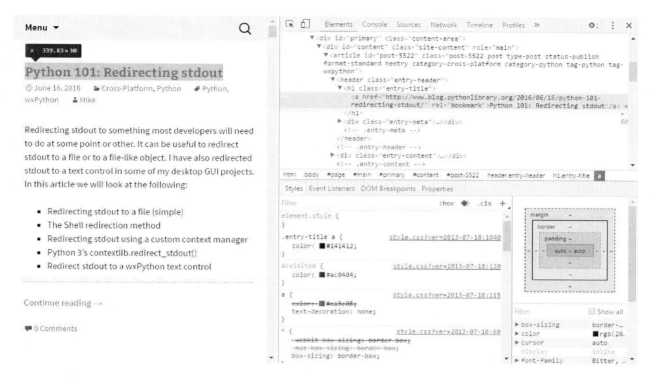

The Mozilla Firefox browser has Developer tools that you can enable on a per page basis that includes an Inspector you can use in much the same way as we did in Chrome. Regardless which web browser you end up using, you will quickly see that the **h1** tag is the one we need to look for. Now that we know what we want to parse, we can learn how to do so!

BeautifulSoup

One of the most popular HTML parsers for Python is called **BeautifulSoup**. It's been around for quite some time and is known for being able to handle malformed HTML well. To install it for Python 3, all you need to do is the following:

```
1  pip install beautifulsoup4
```

If everything worked correctly, you should now have BeautifulSoup installed. When passing BeautifulSoup some HTML to parse, you can specify a tree builder. For this example we will use **html.parser**, because it is included with Python. If you'd like something faster, you can install lxml.

Let's actually take a look at some code to see how this all works:

```
1    import requests
2    from bs4 import BeautifulSoup
3
4
5    url = 'http://www.blog.pythonlibrary.org/'
6
7    def get_articles():
8        """
9        Get the articles from the front page of the blog
10       """
11       req = requests.get(url)
12       html = req.text
13       soup = BeautifulSoup(html, 'html.parser')
14       pages = soup.findAll('h1')
15
16       articles = {i.a['href']: i.text.strip()
17                   for i in pages if i.a}
18       for article in articles:
19           s = '{title}: {url}'.format(
20               title=articles[article],
21               url=article)
22           print(s)
23
24       return articles
25
26   if __name__ == '__main__':
27       articles = get_articles()
```

Here we do out imports and set up what URL we are going to use. Then we create a function where the magic happens. We use the requests library to get the URL and then pull the HTML out as a string using the request object's **text** property. Then we pass the HTML to BeautifulSoup which turns it into a nice object. After that, we ask BeautifulSoup to find all the instances of **h1** and then use a dictionary comprehension to extract the title and URL. We then print that information to stdout and return the dictionary.

Let's try to scrape another website. This time we will look at Twitter and use my blog's account: mousevspython. We will try to scrape what I have tweeted recently. You will need to follow the same steps as before by right-clicking on a tweet and inspecting it to figure out what we need to do. In this case, we need to look for the 'li' tag and the js-stream-item class. Let's take a look:

```
1   import requests
2
3   from bs4 import BeautifulSoup
4
5   url = 'https://twitter.com/mousevspython'
6   req = requests.get(url)
7   html = req.text
8   soup = BeautifulSoup(html, 'html.parser')
9   tweets = soup.findAll('li', 'js-stream-item')
10  for item in range(len(soup.find_all('p', 'TweetTextSize'))):
11      tweet_text = tweets[item].get_text()
12      print(tweet_text)
13      dt = tweets[item].find('a', 'tweet-timestamp')
14      print('This was tweeted on ' + dt)
```

As before, we use BeautifulSoup's **findAll** command to grab all the instances that match our search criteria. Then we also look for the paragraph tag (i.e. 'p') and the 'TweetTextSize' class and loop over the results. You will note that we used **find_all** here. Just so we're clear, findAll is an alias of find_all, so they do the exact same thing. Anyway, we loop over those results and grab the tweet text and the tweet timestamp and print them out.

You would think that there might be an easier way to do this sort of thing and there is. Some websites provide a developer API that you can use to access their website's data. Twitter has a nice one that requires a consumer key and a secret. We will actually be looking at how to use that API and a couple of others in the next chapter.

Let's move on and learn how to write a spider!

Scrapy

Scrapy is a framework that you can use for crawling websites and extracting (i.e. scraping) data. It can also be used to extract data via a website's API or as a general purpose web crawler. To install Scrapy, all you need is pip:

```
1   pip install scrapy
```

According to Scrapy's documentation, you will also need lxml and OpenSSL installed. We are going to use Scrapy to do the same thing that we used BeautifulSoup for, which was scraping the title and link of the articles on my blog's front page. To get started, all you need to do open up a terminal and change directories to the one that you want to store our project in. Then run the following command:

```
1  scrapy startproject blog_scraper
```

This will create a directory named **blog_scraper** in the current directory which will contain the following items:

- Another nested blog_scraper folder
- scrapy.cfg

Inside of the second blog_scraper folder is where the good stuff is:

- A spiders folder
- __init__.py
- items.py
- pipelines.py
- settings.py

We can go with the defaults for everything except **items.py**. So open up **items.py** in your favorite Python editor and add the following code:

```
1  import scrapy
2
3
4  class BlogScraperItem(scrapy.Item):
5      title = scrapy.Field()
6      link = scrapy.Field()
```

What we are doing here is creating a class that models what it is that we want to capture, which in this case is a series of titles and links. This is kind of like SQLAlchemy's model system in which we would create a model of a database. In Scrapy, we create a model of the data we want to scrape.

Next we need to create a spider, so change directories into the **spiders** directory and create a Python file there. Let's just call it **blog.py**. Put the following code inside of your newly created file:

```
1   from scrapy.spider import BaseSpider
2   from scrapy.selector import Selector
3   from ..items import BlogScraperItem
4
5
6   class MyBlogSpider(BaseSpider):
7       name = 'mouse'
8       start_urls = ['http://blog.pythonlibrary.org']
9
10      def parse(self, response):
11          selector = Selector(response)
12          blog_titles = selector.xpath("//h1[@class='entry-title']")
13          selections = []
14
15          for data in blog_titles:
16              selection = BlogScraperItem()
17              selection['title'] = data.xpath("a/text()").extract()
18              selection['link'] = data.xpath("a/@href").extract()
19              selections.append(selection)
20
21          return selections
```

Here we just import the **BaseSpider** class and a **Selector** class. We also import our **BlogScraperItem** class that we created earlier. Then we subclass BaseSpider and name our spider **mouse** since the name of my blog is The Mouse Vs the Python. We also give it a start URL. Note that this is a list which means that you could give this spider multiple start URLs. The most important piece is our **parse** function. It will take the responses it gets from the website and parse them.

Scrapy supports using CSS expressions or XPath for selecting certain parts of an HTML document. This basically tells Scrapy what it is that we want to scrape. XPath is a bit harder to read, but it's also the most powerful, so we'll be using it for this example. To grab the titles, we can use Google Chrome's Inspector tool to figure out that the titles are located inside an **h1** tag with a class name of **entry-title**.

The selector returns an a **SelectorList** instance that we can iterate over. This allows us to continue to make xpath queries on each item in this special list, so we can extract the title text and the link. We also create a new instance of our BlogScraperItem and insert the title and link that we extracted into that new object. Finally we append our newly scraped data into a list which we return when we're done.

To run this code, go back up to the top level folder which contained the nested blog_scraper folder and config file and run the following command:

```
1  scrapy crawl mouse
```

You will notice that we are telling Scrapy to crawl using the **mouse** spider that we created. This command will cause a lot of output to be printed to your screen. Fortunately, Scrapy supports exporting the data into various formats such as CSV, JSON and XML. Let's export the data we scraped using the CSV format:

```
1  scrapy crawl mouse -o articles.csv -t csv
```

You will still see a lot of output generated to stdout, but the title and link will be saved to disk in a file called **articles.csv**.

Most crawlers are set up to follow links and crawl the entire website or a series of websites. The crawler in this website wasn't created that way, but that would be a fun enhancement that you can add on your own.

Wrapping Up

Scraping data from the internet is challenging and fun. Python has many libraries that can make this chore quite easy. We learned about how we can use BeautifulSoup to scrape data from a blog and from Twitter. Then we learned about one of the most popular libraries for creating a web crawler / scraper in Python: Scrapy. We barely scratched the surface of what these libraries can do, so you are encouraged to spend some time reading their respective documentation for further details.

Chapter 20 - Web APIs

As you know the internet is full of fun and interesting websites. A lot of clever programmers have taken advantage of all this free data to create more fun and interesting websites! There are many companies that provide an API or Application Program Interface that you can use to programmatically interact with their websites. There are lots of websites that even provide a Python-specific API that makes interacting with them even easier.

For those that don't, you will have to find alternate ways to interact with them. One of the popular generic interfaces is called Representational State Transfer or REST, which utilizes the HTTP protocol. Another popular API is called Simple Object Access Protocol or SOAP. The SOAP protocol isn't as popular as it used to be, so you will most likely need to learn REST. Feel free to check out SOAP too if you'd like.

This chapter will be focusing on Python wrappers of APIs. We will look briefly at how to extract data from Twitter, Reddit and Wikipedia in this chapter.

As I mentioned in the previous chapter, be sure to read each website's Terms and Conditions. There are usually some limitations to their APIs that you need to keep in mind. Use common sense and don't hit their servers hard with queries or they might revoke your access.

Twitter

Some companies will actually release language specific API wrappers for their API, while others will just publish an API and an independent group will wrap their API in their programming language of choice. In Twitter's case, they just published an API and several different individuals have wrapped it with Python. One of the most popular Python wrappers for the Twitter API is called **tweepy**. Let's install it and give tweepy a try!

```
1  pip install tweepy
```

Now that you have it installed, you will need to register with Twitter to get an authentication key and secret that you can use with their OAuth implementation. Twitter will also provide you with a unique access token and secret for accessing their API. Once you have those in hand we can write some code to extract the tweets from your account. Here's a simple example:

```
1   import tweepy
2
3
4   key = 'random_key'
5   secret = 'random_secret'
6   access_token = 'access_token'
7   access_secret = 'super_secret'
8
9   auth = tweepy.OAuthHandler(key, secret)
10  auth.set_access_token(access_token, access_secret)
11  api = tweepy.API(auth)
12
13  my_tweets = api.user_timeline()
14  for tweet in my_tweets:
15      print(tweet.text)
```

The first few lines of code are all setup. We need to import tweepy and set up our various keys and secrets. Then we can create our authentication handler set our access token. Once that's done, we create a Twitter API object and use that grab our tweets via the **user_timeline** method. You can pass the user_timeline a userid or screen name parameter to get a specific user's tweets. When you don't pass anything, you will get the authenticated user's timeline tweets. Also note that this only returns the 20 latest tweets by default. We can tell it to grab more than that and we can also enable pagination.

In the last chapter, we were also grabbing the date of the tweet with BeautifulSoup. You can do that quite easily by accessing your **tweet** object's **create_at** attribute. If you'd like to know what other items you can access, just call Python's built-in **dir** method on a tweet object:

```
1   >>> dir(tweet)
2   ['__class__', '__delattr__', '__dict__', '__dir__', '__doc__', '__eq__', '__form\
3   at__', '__ge__', '__getattribute__', '__getstate__', '__gt__', '__hash__', '__in\
4   it__', '__le__', '__lt__', '__module__', '__ne__', '__new__', '__reduce__', '__r\
5   educe_ex__', '__repr__', '__setattr__', '__sizeof__', '__str__', '__subclasshook\
6   __', '__weakref__', '_api', '_json', 'author', 'contributors', 'coordinates', 'c\
7   reated_at', 'destroy', 'entities', 'favorite', 'favorite_count', 'favorited', 'g\
8   eo', 'id', 'id_str', 'in_reply_to_screen_name', 'in_reply_to_status_id', 'in_rep\
9   ly_to_status_id_str', 'in_reply_to_user_id', 'in_reply_to_user_id_str', 'is_quot\
10  e_status', 'lang', 'parse', 'parse_list', 'place', 'possibly_sensitive', 'retwee\
11  t', 'retweet_count', 'retweeted', 'retweets', 'source', 'source_url', 'text', 't\
12  runcated', 'user']
```

You can actually update your status via the api object we created:

```
1  >>> api.update_status('I just tweeted using Python')
2  >>> api.update_with_media(filename, 'I can tweet files with Python')
```

Basically you can do just about anything with tweepy that you can do in a browser on Twitter. I highly recommend checking out their documentation as there is a lot more to their API than what I can cover in this chapter.

Reddit

Reddit is a very popular entertainment and social new networking service. It's kind of like Slashdot in that users vote on which stories are the best and they can get promoted to the front page. A few years ago, Digg used to be the big site that did this sort of thing. Reddit has lots of sub-sites called subreddits that are devoted to specific subjects, like gaming, photos, programming languages, etc.

Reddit also has published an API that has been wrapped by some clever Python programmers. It is called **PRAW: The Python Reddit Api Wrapper**. We can install PRAW using pip:

```
1  pip install praw
```

Now that we have that installed, let's give praw a try. We will try getting the top 25 stories on Reddit right now:

```
1  >>> import praw
2  >>> red = praw.Reddit(user_agent='pyred')
3  >>> red.get_top()
4  <generator object get_content at 0x7fab626b6620>
5  >>> for i in red.get_top():
6  ...     print(i)
7  ...
8  6807 :: Supreme Court Strikes Down Strict Abortion Law
9  5583 :: Grandpa plays a virtual reality game
10 5532 :: Our trip to the petting zoo did not go as planned
11 5728 :: My pepper looks like a fist
12 5501 :: New Samurai Jack receives a TV-MA rating for it's dark tone and viole...
13 5868 :: The sunset at Glastonbury Festival on Saturday was incredible.
14 5485 :: Let me out of this kennel please!
15 5427 :: Good morning, I love you!
16 5389 :: TIL an airplane crashed into the Empire State Building in 1945. Among...
17 5409 :: Meanwhile in France...
18 5340 :: Barclays and RBS shares suspended from trading after tanking more tha...
19 5228 :: The wood grain on this door looks like a damp woman ran into it
```

```
20  5225 :: Seeing a ceiling fan in action for the first time
21  5258 :: Half funny, half disturbing
22  5067 :: Old dogs are cute too.
23  5036 :: Our veterinary clinic sent us a sympathy card with our dog's paw prin...
24  5082 :: Experiments confirm that the barium-144 nucleus is pear shaped
25  5340 :: He doesn't like his new bow tie
26  4924 :: One of my favorite jokes from Dr. Cox.
27  4921 :: Pope says Church should ask forgiveness from gays for past treatment
28  4912 :: Hawaii becomes first U.S. state to place gun owners on FBI database
29  5043 :: I'll give a million dollars to the man who can do something about mot...
30  4836 :: 100 kids have sleepover at Dallas Cowboys' AT&T Stadium as part of As...
31  4719 :: TIL illegal income, such as bribes, are considered taxable income. Au...
32  4681 :: War Veteran, pencil on paper, A2
```

Here we just imported the **praw** module and created a **Reddit** instance. You will note that we set the user_agent to a custom string. You can basically set the string to anything you want. Next up, we call **get_top** to grab the current top 25 articles. This returns a generator, so we loop over said generator and print out each item.

Most people like browsing Reddit's subreddits. So let's find out how we can do that next!

```
1   >>> python = red.get_subreddit('python')
2   >>> submissions = python.get_hot(limit=5)
3   >>> submissions
4   <generator object get_content at 0x7fab632614c0>
5   >>> for submission in submissions:
6   ...     print(submission)
7   ...
8   298 :: Post learning questions to /r/LearnPython
9   146 :: Python 3.5.2 is released
10  84 :: My peer-to-peer networking module is now on pip
11  36 :: WTF! Stop the next line
12  0 :: [Advice] What path should I choose for further programming?
```

In this example, we just call the **get_subreddit** method and tell it we want the **python** subreddit. This call returnds a **Subreddit** object, so we call its **get_hot** method and tell it to give us the top 5 results. This too is a generator object, so we quickly write a loop to iterate over the submissions and print them out.

A lot of people enjoy the comments on a submission as much or more than the submission itself. If you happen to open a submission, you will note in the URL that it has a unique identifier such as **4q2lxb**. This is the submission id. We can use that information to get a **Submission** object!

```
1  >>> id = '4q2lxb'
2  >>> submission = red.get_submission(submission_id=id)
3  >>> comments = submission.comments
4  >>> comments
5  [<praw.objects.Comment object at 0x7fab626c2668>]
6  >>> comments[0].author
7  Redditor(user_name='brombaer3000')
8  >>> comments[0].body
9  ('[Actual release '
10  'notes](https://docs.python.org/3/whatsnew/changelog.html#python-3-5-2)')
11  >>> comments[0].replies
12  [<praw.objects.Comment object at 0x7fab626c2588>]
```

I ended up clicking on a submission about the latest release of Python for this example and its id was **4q2lxb**. So here we just call our API object's **get_submission** method and pass it the id we want to look up. Then you can grab the comments via the **comments** property of the Submission object. This returns a list of Comment objects. You can loop over the list or you can just access specific items from the list to see what they contain. We go with the latter approach here and print out the author of the comment along with its body. We also check to see if anyone replied to the comment by accessing the comment's **replies** property which also returns a list of Comment objects.

I highly recommend spending some time looking over the documentation for PRAW as it is a very interesting little package. You can use Python's introspection capabilities to learn a lot too. For example, you should try calling **dir** on a Submission or Comment object to see what all you can access.

Wikipedia

Wikipedia is free crowd-sourced encyclopedia. It is constantly updated and has millions of articles. Wikipedia also has a simple API that's been wrapped for Python in the **wikipedia** package. Let's install it and see how we might use it!

```
1  pip install wikipedia
```

The wikipedia package depends on BeautifulSoup and the requests package. Fortunately, it will install them or upgrade them itself if they are missing or out-of-date. Now that we have wikipedia installed, let's try asking it what it knows about the Python:

```
1  >>> import wikipedia
2  >>> wikipedia.search('Python')
3  ['Python',
4   'Python (programming language)',
5   'Python molurus',
6   'Webware for Python',
7   'List of pythonid species and subspecies',
8   'African rock python',
9   'Python (missile)',
10  'Borneo Python',
11  'Reticulated python',
12  'Python for S60']
```

Well, that was slightly unexpected. If we just search for the word "Python" on Wikipedia, it is going to return a list of items. So we need to be more specific. That second item in the list looks like the one we want, so let's try grabbing its **summary** information:

```
1  >>> wikipedia.summary('Python (programming language)')
2  ('Python is a widely used high-level, general-purpose, interpreted, dynamic '
3   'programming language. Its design philosophy emphasizes code readability, and '
4   'its syntax allows programmers to express concepts in fewer lines of code '
5   'than possible in languages such as C++ or Java. The language provides '
6   'constructs intended to enable clear programs on both a small and large '
7   'scale.\n'
8   'Python supports multiple programming paradigms, including object-oriented, '
9   'imperative and functional programming or procedural styles. It features a '
10  'dynamic type system and automatic memory management and has a large and '
11  'comprehensive standard library.\n'
12  'Python interpreters are available for many operating systems, allowing '
13  'Python code to run on a wide variety of systems. Using third-party tools, '
14  'such as Py2exe or Pyinstaller, Python code can be packaged into stand-alone '
15  'executable programs for some of the most popular operating systems, so '
16  'Python-based software can be distributed to, and used on, those environments '
17  'with no need to install a Python interpreter.\n'
18  'CPython, the reference implementation of Python, is free and open-source '
19  'software and has a community-based development model, as do nearly all of '
20  'its variant implementations. CPython is managed by the non-profit Python '
21  'Software Foundation.')
```

That looks better. Now we know how to grab summary information about something that we searched, so let's use that knowledge to make a function we can use to query Wikipedia:

```
1   import wikipedia
2
3
4   def print_wikipedia_results(word):
5       """
6       Searches for pages that match the specified word
7       """
8       results = wikipedia.search(word)
9
10      for result in results:
11          try:
12              page = wikipedia.page(result)
13          except wikipedia.exceptions.DisambiguationError:
14              print('DisambiguationError')
15              continue
16          except wikipedia.exceptions.PageError:
17              print('PageError for result: ' + result)
18              continue
19
20          print(page.summary)
21
22  if __name__ == '__main__':
23      print_wikipedia_results('wombat')
```

Our function, **print_wikipedia_results**, takes in the word or phrase that we'd like to look up and returns a list of results. We then loop over the results and attempt to create a **WikipediaPage** instance. However if you pass an ambiguous word or phrase to the **page** method, then it will raise a **DisambiguationError**. So we catch that and ignore it. We also catch **PageErrors**, although you might want to just raise an error on those as they seem a bit more serious. When we do get a valid WikipediaPage object back though, we go ahead and print out its summary.

Let's look briefly at some of the properties we can access on our WikipediaPage object:

```
1   >>> page = wikipedia.page('Python (programming language)')
2   >>> page
3   <WikipediaPage 'Python (programming language)'>
4   >>> page.title
5   'Python (programming language)'
6   >>> page.url
7   'https://en.wikipedia.org/wiki/Python_(programming_language)'
8   >>> page.content
9   ('Python is a widely used high-level, general-purpose, interpreted, dynamic ' ...
```

Here we show how you can get the title, url and content of the article. You can also get the links, images, html and more too.

Another fun feature of the wikipedia package is that it allows you to set what language the results should be in. Let's take a look:

```
1   >>> wikipedia.set_lang("fr")
2   None
3   >>> page = wikipedia.page('Python (programming language)')
4   >>> page.summary
5   ('Python est un langage de programmation objet, multi-paradigme et '
6    'multiplateformes. Il favorise la programmation impérative structurée, '
7    "fonctionnelle et orientée objet. Il est doté d'un typage dynamique fort, "
8    "d'une gestion automatique de la mémoire par ramasse-miettes et d'un système "
9    "de gestion d'exceptions ; il est ainsi similaire à Perl, Ruby, Scheme, "
10   'Smalltalk et Tcl.\n'
11   'Le langage Python est placé sous une licence libre proche de la licence BSD '
12   'et fonctionne sur la plupart des plates-formes informatiques, des '
13   'supercalculateurs aux ordinateurs centraux, de Windows à Unix en passant par '
14   'GNU/Linux, Mac OS, ou encore Android, iOS, et aussi avec Java ou encore '
15   '.NET. Il est conçu pour optimiser la productivité des programmeurs en '
16   'offrant des outils de haut niveau et une syntaxe simple à utiliser.\n'
17   'Il est également apprécié par les pédagogues qui y trouvent un langage où la '
18   'syntaxe, clairement séparée des mécanismes de bas niveau, permet une '
19   'initiation aisée aux concepts de base de la programmation.')
```

Here we told the wikipedia package that we want the language to be French, then we grabbed the summary of our Python page again. As you can see, it's now in French.

Other API Libraries

There are many, many other websites that have provided support for Python or that have Python wrappers around their APIs. Google itself provides a Python API called the **Google API Python Client** that gives you access to a lot of Google's services. It uses OAuth for authentication, but is pretty full featured. The API documentation is good but it doesn't include very many Python examples.

Amazon published a library for their Web Services (AWS) that they call Boto3. You can use Boto for writing software that utilizes Amazon's S3 and EC2, among others. They have published documentation that has lots of brief examples.

If the website is popular and contains lots of data, it probably has some kind of Python wrapper that you can use.

Wrapping Up

We covered a lot of information in this chapter. You should now know how to access Twitter, Reddit and Wikipedia using various Python packages. You can now create your own clients for these popular websites should you so desire. It would be fun to add some kind of user interface to you client. If you decide to go that route, you might want to check out Tkinter, wxPython or Kivy.

Chapter 21 - Working with FTP

The File Transfer Protocol (FTP) is used by many companies and organizations for sharing data. Python provides an File Transfer Protocol module in its standard library called **ftplib** that implements the client side of the FTP protocol. You can learn all about the File Transfer Protocol by reading the RFC 959 document on the Internet. However the full specification is outside the scope of this chapter. Instead we will focus on the following topics:

- Connecting to an FTP server
- Navigating it's structure
- Downloading files from the FTP server
- Uploading files to an FTP server

Let's get started!

Connecting to an FTP Server

The first thing we need to do is find an FTP server to connect to. There are many free ones you can use. For example, most Linux distributions have FTP mirrors that are publicly accessible. If you go to Fedora's website (https://admin.fedoraproject.org/mirrormanager/) you will find a long list of mirrors that you can use. They aren't just FTP though, so be sure that you choose the correct protocol or you will receive a connection error.

For this example, we will use **ftp.cse.buffalo.edu**. The official Python documentation uses **ftp.debian.org**, so feel free to try that as well. Let's try to connect to the server now. Open up the Python interpreter in your terminal or use IDLE to follow along:

```
1  >>> from ftplib import FTP
2  >>> ftp = FTP('ftp.cse.buffalo.edu')
3  >>> ftp.login()
4  '230 Guest login ok, access restrictions apply.'
```

Let's break this down a bit. Here we import the **FTP** class from ftplib. Then we create an instance of the class by passing it the host that we want to connect to. Since we did not pass a username or password, Python assumes we want to login anonymously. If you happen to need to connect to the FTP server using a non-standard port, then you can do so using the **connect** method. Here's how:

```
1  >>> from ftplib import FTP
2  >>> ftp = FTP()
3  >>> HOST = 'ftp.cse.buffalo.edu'
4  >>> PORT = 12345
5  >>> ftp.connect(HOST, PORT)
```

This code will fail as the FTP server in this example doesn't have port 12345 open for us. However, the idea is to convey how to connect to a port that differs from the default.

If the FTP server that you're connecting to requires TLS security, then you will want to import the **FTP_TLS** class instead of the **FTP** class. The **FTP_TLS** class supports a keyfile and a certfile. If you want to secure your connection, then you will need to call **prot_p** to do so.

Navigating Directories with ftplib

Let's learn how to see what's on the FTP server and change directories! Here is some code that demonstrates the normal method of doing so:

```
1  >>> from ftplib import FTP
2  >>> ftp = FTP()
3  >>> ftp.login()
4  >>> ftp.retrlines('LIST')
5  total 28
6  drwxrwxrwx   2 0         0      4096 Sep  6  2015 .snapshot
7  drwxr-xr-x   2 202019    5564   4096 Sep  6  2015 CSE421
8  drwxr-xr-x   2 0         0      4096 Jul 23  2008 bin
9  drwxr-xr-x   2 0         0      4096 Mar 15  2007 etc
10 drwxr-xr-x   6 89987     546    4096 Sep  6  2015 mirror
11 drwxrwxr-x   7 6980      546    4096 Jul  3  2014 pub
12 drwxr-xr-x  26 0         11     4096 Apr 29 20:31 users
13 '226 Transfer complete.'
14 >>> ftp.cwd('mirror')
15 '250 CWD command successful.'
16 >>> ftp.retrlines('LIST')
17 total 16
18 drwxr-xr-x   3 89987     546    4096 Sep  6  2015 BSD
19 drwxr-xr-x   5 89987     546    4096 Sep  6  2015 Linux
20 drwxr-xr-x   4 89987     546    4096 Sep  6  2015 Network
21 drwxr-xr-x   4 89987     546    4096 Sep  6  2015 X11
22 '226 Transfer complete.'
```

Here we get logged in and then we send the LIST command to the FTP server. This is done by calling our ftp object's **retrlines** method. The **retrlines** method prints out the result of the command we called. In this example, we called LIST which retrieves a list of files and/or folders along with their respective informations and prints them out. Then we used the **cwd** command to change our working directory to a different folder and then re-ran the LIST command to see what was in it. You could also use your ftp object's **dir** function to get a listing of the current folder.

Downloading a File via FTP

Just viewing what's on an FTP server isn't all that useful. You will almost always want to download a file from the server. Let's find out how to download a single file:

```
1  >>> from ftplib import FTP
2  >>> ftp = FTP('ftp.debian.org')
3  >>> ftp.login()
4  '230 Login successful.'
5  >>> ftp.cwd('debian')
6  '250 Directory successfully changed.'
7  >>> out = '/home/mike/Desktop/README'
8  >>> with open(out, 'wb') as f:
9  ...     ftp.retrbinary('RETR ' + 'README.html', f.write)
```

For this example, we login to the Debian Linux FTP and change to the debian folder. Then we create the name of the file we want to save to and open it in write-binary mode. Finally we use the ftp object's **retrbinary** to call RETR to retrieve the file and write it to our local disk. If you'd like to download all the files, then we'll need to a file listing.

```
1  import ftplib
2  import os
3
4  ftp = ftplib.FTP('ftp.debian.org')
5  ftp.login()
6  ftp.cwd('debian')
7  filenames = ftp.nlst()
8
9  for filename in filenames:
10     host_file = os.path.join(
11         '/home/mike/Desktop/ftp_test', filename)
12     try:
13         with open(host_file, 'wb') as local_file:
14             ftp.retrbinary('RETR ' + filename, local_file.write)
```

```
15      except ftplib.error_perm:
16          pass
17
18  ftp.quit()
```

This example is fairly similar to the previous one. You will need to modify it to match your own preferred download location though. The first part of the code is pretty much the same, but then you will note that we call **nlst** which gives us a list of filenames and directories. You can give it a directory to list or just call it without and it will assume you want a listing of the current directory. Note that the nlst command doesn't tell us how to differentiate between files and directories from its results. For this example though, we simply don't care. This is more of a brute force script. So it will loop over the list returned and attempt to download them. If the "file" happens to actually be a directory, then we'll end up creating an empty file on our local disk with the same name as the directory on the FTP server.

There is an MLSD command that you can call via the **mlsd** method, but not all FTP servers support this command. If they do, then you might be able to differentiate between the two.

Uploading Files to an FTP Server

The other major task that you do with an FTP server is upload files to it. Python can handle this too. There are actually two methods that you can use for uploading file:

- storlines - Used for uploading text files (TXT, HTML, RST)
- storbinary - Used for uploading binary files (PDF, XLS, etc)

Let's look at an example of how we might do this:

```
1   import ftplib
2
3   def ftp_upload(ftp_obj, path, ftype='TXT'):
4       """
5       A function for uploading files to an FTP server
6       @param ftp_obj: The file transfer protocol object
7       @param path: The path to the file to upload
8       """
9       if ftype == 'TXT':
10          with open(path) as fobj:
11              ftp.storlines('STOR ' + path, fobj)
12      else:
13          with open(path, 'rb') as fobj:
```

```
14              ftp.storbinary('STOR ' + path, fobj, 1024)
15
16  if __name__ == '__main__':
17      ftp = ftplib.FTP('host', 'username', 'password')
18      ftp.login()
19
20      path = '/path/to/something.txt'
21      ftp_upload(ftp, path)
22
23      pdf_path = '/path/to/something.pdf'
24      ftp_upload(ftp, pdf_path, ftype='PDF')
25
26      ftp.quit()
```

In this example, we create a function for uploading files. It takes an ftp object, the path of the file we want to upload and the type of the file. Then we do a quick check on the file type to determine if we should use **storlines** or **storbinary** for our upload process. Finally in our conditional statement at the bottom, we connect to the FTP server, login and upload a text file and a PDF file. An easy enhancement to add to this is some logic for changing to a specific directory once we're logged in as we probably don't want to just upload files to the root location.

Wrapping Up

At this point, you should know enough to get started using Python's ftplib. It has a lot of other methods that are well worth checking out in Python's documentation on the module. But you now know the basics of listing a directory, navigating the folder structure as well as downloading and uploading files.

Chapter 22 - The urllib Module

The **urllib** module in Python 3 is a collection of modules that you can use for working with URLs. If you are coming from a Python 2 background you will note that in Python 2 you had urllib and urllib2. These are now a part of the urllib package in Python 3. The current version of urllib is made up of the following modules:

- urllib.request
- urllib.error
- urllib.parse
- urllib.rebotparser

We will be covering each part individually except for **urllib.error**. The official documentation actually recommends that you might want to check out the 3rd party library, **requests**, for a higher-level HTTP client interface. However, I believe that it can be useful to know how to open URLs and interact with them without using a 3rd party and it may also help you appreciate why the requests package is so popular.

urllib.request

The **urllib.request** module is primarily used for opening and fetching URLs. Let's take a look at some of the things you can do with the **urlopen** function:

```
1  >>> import urllib.request
2  >>> url = urllib.request.urlopen('https://www.google.com/')
3  >>> url.geturl()
4  'https://www.google.com/'
5  >>> url.info()
6  <http.client.HTTPMessage object at 0x7fddc2de04e0>
7  >>> header = url.info()
8  >>> header.as_string()
9  ('Date: Fri, 24 Jun 2016 18:21:19 GMT\n'
10  'Expires: -1\n'
11  'Cache-Control: private, max-age=0\n'
```

```
12    'Content-Type: text/html; charset=ISO-8859-1\n'
13    'P3P: CP="This is not a P3P policy! See '
14    'https://www.google.com/support/accounts/answer/151657?hl=en for more info."\n'
15    'Server: gws\n'
16    'X-XSS-Protection: 1; mode=block\n'
17    'X-Frame-Options: SAMEORIGIN\n'
18    'Set-Cookie: '
19    'NID=80=tYjmy0JY6flsSVj7DPSSZNOuqdvqKfKHDcHsPIGu3xFv41LvH_Jg6LrUsDgkPrtM2hmZ3j9\
20    V76pS4K_cBg7pdwueMQfr0DFzw33SwpGex5qzLkXUvUVPfe9g699Qz4cx9ipcbU3HKwrRYA; '
21    'expires=Sat, 24-Dec-2016 18:21:19 GMT; path=/; domain=.google.com; HttpOnly\n'
22    'Alternate-Protocol: 443:quic\n'
23    'Alt-Svc: quic=":443"; ma=2592000; v="34,33,32,31,30,29,28,27,26,25"\n'
24    'Accept-Ranges: none\n'
25    'Vary: Accept-Encoding\n'
26    'Connection: close\n'
27    '\n')
28 >>> url.getcode()
29 200
```

Here we import our module and ask it to open Google's URL. Now we have an **HTTPResponse** object that we can interact with. The first thing we do is call the **geturl** method which will return the URL of the resource that was retrieved. This is useful for finding out if we followed a redirect.

Next we call **info**, which will return meta-data about the page, such as headers. Because of this, we assign that result to our **headers** variable and then call its **as_string** method. This prints out the header we received from Google. You can also get the HTTP response code by calling **getcode**, which in this case was 200, which means it worked successfully.

If you'd like to see the HTML of the page, you can call the **read** method on the url variable we created. I am not reproducing that here as the output will be quite long.

Please note that the request object defaults to a GET request unless you specify the **data** parameter. Should you pass in the data parameter, then the request object will issue a POST request instead.

Downloading a File

A typical use case for the urllib package is for downloading a file. Let's find out a couple of ways we can accomplish this task:

```
1  >>> import urllib.request
2  >>> url = 'http://www.blog.pythonlibrary.org/wp-content/uploads/2012/06/wxDbView\
3  er.zip'
4  >>> response = urllib.request.urlopen(url)
5  >>> data = response.read()
6  >>> with open('/home/mike/Desktop/test.zip', 'wb') as fobj:
7  ...      fobj.write(data)
8  ...
```

Here we just open a URL that leads us to a zip file stored on my blog. Then we read the data and write it out to disk. An alternate way to accomplish this is to use **urlretrieve**:

```
1  >>> import urllib.request
2  >>> url = 'http://www.blog.pythonlibrary.org/wp-content/uploads/2012/06/wxDbView\
3  er.zip'
4  >>> tmp_file, header = urllib.request.urlretrieve(url)
5  >>> with open('/home/mike/Desktop/test.zip', 'wb') as fobj:
6  ...      with open(tmp_file, 'rb') as tmp:
7  ...          fobj.write(tmp.read())
```

The urlretrieve method will copy a network object to a local file. The file it copies to is randomly named and goes into the temp directory unless you use the second parameter to urlretrieve where you can actually specify where you want the file saved. This will save you a step and make your code much simpler:

```
1  >>> import urllib.request
2  >>> url = 'http://www.blog.pythonlibrary.org/wp-content/uploads/2012/06/wxDbView\
3  er.zip'
4  >>> urllib.request.urlretrieve(url, '/home/mike/Desktop/blog.zip')
5  ('/home/mike/Desktop/blog.zip',
6   <http.client.HTTPMessage object at 0x7fddc21c2470>)
```

As you can see, it returns the location of where it saved the file and the header information from the request.

Specifying Your User Agent

When you visit a website with your browser, the browser tells the website who it is. This is called the **user-agent** string. Python's urllib identifies itself as **Python-urllib/x.y** where the x and y are major and minor version numbers of Python. Some websites won't recognize this user-agent string and will behave in strange ways or not work at all. Fortunately, it's easy for you to set up your own custom user-agent string:

```
1  >>> import urllib.request
2  >>> user_agent = ' Mozilla/5.0 (X11; Ubuntu; Linux x86_64; rv:47.0) Gecko/201001\
3  01 Firefox/47.0'
4  >>> url = 'http://www.whatsmyua.com/'
5  >>> headers = {'User-Agent': user_agent}
6  >>> request = urllib.request.Request(url, headers=headers)
7  >>> with urllib.request.urlopen(request) as response:
8  ...     with open('/home/mdriscoll/Desktop/user_agent.html', 'wb') as out:
9  ...         out.write(response.read())
```

Here we set up our user agent to Mozilla FireFox and we set out URL to **http://www.whatsmyua. com/** which will tell us what it thinks our user-agent string is. Then we create aRequest** instance using our url and headers and pass that to **urlopen**. Finally we save the result. If you open the result file, you will see that we successfully changed our user-agent string. Feel free to try out a few different strings with this code to see how it will change.

urllib.parse

The **urllib.parse** library is your standard interface for breaking up URL strings and combining them back together. You can use it to convert a relative URL to an absolute URL, for example. Let's try using it to parse a URL that includes a query:

```
1  >>> from urllib.parse import urlparse
2  >>> result = urlparse('https://duckduckgo.com/?q=python+stubbing&t=canonical&ia=\
3  qa')
4  >>> result
5  ParseResult(scheme='https', netloc='duckduckgo.com', path='/', params='', query=\
6  'q=python+stubbing&t=canonical&ia=qa', fragment='')
7  >>> result.netloc
8  'duckduckgo.com'
9  >>> result.geturl()
10 'https://duckduckgo.com/?q=python+stubbing&t=canonical&ia=qa'
11 >>> result.port
12 None
```

Here we import the **urlparse** function and pass it an URL that contains a search query to the duckduckgo website. My query was to look up articles on "python stubbing". As you can see, it returned a **ParseResult** object that you can use to learn more about the URL. For example, you can get the port information (None in this case), the network location, path and much more.

Submitting a Web Form

This module also holds the **urlencode** method, which is great for passing data to a URL. A typical use case for the urllib.parse library is submitting a web form. Let's find out how you might do that by having the duckduckgo search engine look for Python:

```
1  >>> import urllib.request
2  >>> import urllib.parse
3  >>> data = urllib.parse.urlencode({'q': 'Python'})
4  >>> data
5  'q=Python'
6  >>> url = 'http://duckduckgo.com/html/'
7  >>> full_url = url + '?' + data
8  >>> response = urllib.request.urlopen(full_url)
9  >>> with open('/home/mike/Desktop/results.html', 'wb') as f:
10 ...     f.write(response.read())
```

This is pretty straightforward. Basically we want to submit a query to duckduckgo ourselves using Python instead of a browser. To do that, we need to construct our query string using **urlencode**. Then we put that together to create a fully qualified URL and use urllib.request to submit the form. We then grab the result and save it to disk.

urllib.robotparser

The **robotparser** module is made up of a single class, **RobotFileParser**. This class will answer questions about whether or not a specific user agent can fetch a URL that has a published **robot.txt** file. The robots.txt file will tell a web scraper or robot what parts of the server should not be accessed. Let's take a look at a simple example using ArsTechnica's website:

```
1  >>> import urllib.robotparser
2  >>> robot = urllib.robotparser.RobotFileParser()
3  >>> robot.set_url('http://arstechnica.com/robots.txt')
4  None
5  >>> robot.read()
6  None
7  >>> robot.can_fetch('*', 'http://arstechnica.com/')
8  True
9  >>> robot.can_fetch('*', 'http://arstechnica.com/cgi-bin/')
10 False
```

Here we import the robot parser class and create an instance of it. Then we pass it a URL that specifies where the website's robots.txt file resides. Next we tell our parser to read the file. Now that that's done, we give it a couple of different URLs to find out which ones we can crawl and which ones we can't. We quickly see that we can access the main site, but not the cgi-bin.

Wrapping Up

You have reached the point that you should be able to use Python's urllib package competently. We learned how to download a file, submit a web form, change our user agent and access a robots.txt file in this chapter. The urllib has a lot of additional functionality that is not covered here, such as website authentication. However, you might want to consider switching to the **requests** library before trying to do authentication with urllib as the requests implementation is a lot easier to understand and debug. I also want to note that Python has support for Cookies via its **http.cookies** module although that is also wrapped quite well in the requests package. You should probably consider trying both to see which one makes the most sense to you.

Part IV - Testing

Welcome to part IV! In this section, we will take a quick look at some of Python's built-in testing modules. These are great tools to have to help you make sure you are writing quality code. We will also be looking at a useful 3rd party module called **coverage.py**. Here is a list of the specifics:

- Chapter 23 - The doctest module
- Chapter 24 - The unittest module
- Chapter 25 - The unittest.mock module
- Chapter 26 - coverage.py

By learning how to use these modules and packages effectively, you will be able to test your code successfully and know what parts may not have the best test coverage.

Let's get cracking!

Chapter 24 - The doctest Module

Python includes a really useful module in its standard library that is called **doctest**. The doctest module will look at your code and determine if you have any text that looks like an interactive Python session. Then doctest will execute those strings to verify that they work the way they are written.

According to the Python documentation, doctest has three primary uses:

- Checking that a module's docstrings are up-to-date by verifying the examples in the docstrings execute correctly
- Do regression testing using the interactive examples in the text or
- Write tutorial documentation for your package or module. You can do this by adding lots of examples in your docstrings that show inputs and outputs.

Let's create a simple addition function that we can use to demonstrate what you might do with doctest. Save the following code into a file named **mymath.py**:

```python
def add(a, b):
    """
    Return the addition of the arguments: a + b

    >>> add(1, 2)
    3
    >>> add(-1, 10)
    9
    >>> add('a', 'b')
    'ab'
    >>> add(1, '2')
    Traceback (most recent call last):
      File "test.py", line 17, in <module>
        add(1, '2')
      File "test.py", line 14, in add
        return a + b
    TypeError: unsupported operand type(s) for +: 'int' and 'str'
```

```
18        """
19        return a + b
20
21    if __name__ == '__main__':
22        import doctest
23        doctest.testmod()
```

You will notice that we have a very large docstring here with what appears to be a session from the Python interpreter. This is exactly what you want to do when you write your docstrings for doctest. You can run your function in the Python interpreter or IDLE and test it out. Then you can take some of the examples you tried along with its output and add it to your function's docstring. At the very end of this example, we import doctest and call its **testmod** function. The testmod() call will then search all the docstrings in the module and try to run the examples that look like interpreter sessions.

Let's try running this code to see what kind of output we get.

```
1    mike@mac: python test.py
```

You will notice that all we need to do is call Python and pass it our test script. When you run this code, you shouldn't see any output whatsoever. That means the test passed. If you want to actually see some output, then you will need to enable verbose mode by passing in **-v**:

```
1    mike@mac-028: python3 test.py -v
2    Trying:
3        add(1, 2)
4    Expecting:
5        3
6    ok
7    Trying:
8        add(-1, 10)
9    Expecting:
10       9
11   ok
12   Trying:
13       add('a', 'b')
14   Expecting:
15       'ab'
16   ok
17   Trying:
18       add(1, '2')
19   Expecting:
```

```
20    Traceback (most recent call last):
21      File "docked.py", line 17, in <module>
22        add(1, '2')
23      File "docked.py", line 14, in add
24        return a + b
25    TypeError: unsupported operand type(s) for +: 'int' and 'str'
26  ok
27  1 items had no tests:
28      __main__
29  1 items passed all tests:
30      4 tests in __main__.add
31  4 tests in 2 items.
32  4 passed and 0 failed.
33  Test passed.
```

As the last line indicates, our test ran 4 tests and they all passed. There's another way to call doctest on a module that is only on the command line. You will need to modify the example from earlier to remove the if statement at the end so that your script now only contains the function. Then you can run the following:

```
1  python -m doctest -v test.py
```

This command tells Python to run the doctest module in verbose mode against the script we created.

How it Works

The doctest module works by examining the docstrings in the module, from the module level to the function, class and method levels. It will not look at imported modules though. For the most part, you can copy-and-paste an interactive console session in and doctest will work fine with it.

doctest will look for output following the final >>> or ... line that contains code. Said output will only extend to the next >>> or all-whitespace line.

Here are a few gotcha's to watch out for.

- If you continue a line using a backslash, then you will want to use a raw docstring (i.e. r"""This is raw""") to preserve the backslash. Otherwise it will be considered a part of the string and will probably raise an error.
- Tracebacks usually contain exact file path and line numbers which change when you're developing and will the paths will certainly change across machines. So this will cause issues too. Fortunately, doctest is pretty flexible with tracebacks. You only need the Traceback line and the actual Exception line to make the test pass. Just change the example from before to this:

```
1   def add(a, b):
2       """
3       Return the addition of the arguments: a + b
4
5       >>> add(1, 2)
6       3
7       >>> add(-1, 10)
8       9
9       >>> add('a', 'b')
10      'ab'
11      >>> add(1, '2')
12      Traceback (most recent call last):
13      TypeError: unsupported operand type(s) for +: 'int' and 'str'
14      """
15      return a + b
```

- As you know dictionaries don't have a specific ordering, so if you try to print one in your doctest, it will probably fail. Instead, if you must use a dictionary, you should do a comparison of dictionaries as that should return a bool and be much more reliable.
- The same issue arises when you print an **id** or an instance of something, like a class. Since these are dynamic, they won't work well with doctest.

Check Your Test With a Text File

The doctest module also allows you to write interactive examples to a text file using ReStructured-Text, which is a common mark-up language. Let's create a really simple example. Save the following in the same folder as you did for our add function above and be sure to name it **add.txt**:

```
1   =====================
2   The ``add`` function
3   =====================
4
5   --------------------
6   How to use ``add``
7   --------------------
8
9   The ``add`` function needs to be imported from the **mymath** module like this:
10
11      >>> from mymath import add
12
```

```
13  Now you can use ``add`` to add various data types together, such as integers, fl\
14  oats, strings, and more. Here's an example:
15
16      >>> add(1, 2)
17      3
```

The example above explains what we are doing, which is basically importing the add function from our mymath module and then testing it out. Now we need to actually write a test script to run our test file:

```
1  import doctest
2
3  doctest.testfile('add.txt')
```

Once you have this code in your file, save it with the name **test_mymath.py**. Now we can run this code like so:

```
1  python test_mymath.py -v
```

We add the **-v** flag as before so that it runs the test in verbose mode. You should end up seeing the following output if you didn't make any typos:

```
1  Trying:
2      from mymath import add
3  Expecting nothing
4  ok
5  Trying:
6      add(1, 2)
7  Expecting:
8      3
9  ok
10 1 items passed all tests:
11    2 tests in add.txt
12 2 tests in 1 items.
13 2 passed and 0 failed.
14 Test passed.
```

As you can see, we passed all our tests!

Option Flags and Directives

The doctest module comes with several option flags that you can use to control doctest's behavior. There are quite a few of them, so we well only look at a couple of examples of one flag to show how you might use them. For full details, be sure to read the official documentation on doctest!

One of the easiest ways to use an option flag is with a directive. A doctest directive is a special Python comment that follows an example's source code. One of the most popular option flags to use is the **ELLIPSIS** flag. Let's put the following code into a file and name it **test_directives.py**:

```
1  """
2  >>> print(list(range(100))) # doctest: +ELLIPSIS
3  [0, 1, ..., 98, 99]
4
5  >>> class Dog: pass
6  >>> Dog() #doctest: +ELLIPSIS
7  <__main__.Dog object at 0x...>
8  """
9
10 if __name__ == '__main__':
11     import doctest
12     doctest.testmod()
```

The ELLIPSIS flag allows us to cut out part of the output and still pass the test. For the first example, we create a list with 100 elements, 0-99. Since this is a lot of data that we don't want to store in our docstring, we use the ELLIPSIS option flag. This allows us to put an ellipsis in the middle of the result to represent the values that we're not showing.

In the second example, we want to create an instance of the Dog class, which will return an object with a name that changes every time you run this test. Since we can't put something dynamic into our doctest, we can use the ELLIPSIS option flag to tell doctest to ignore most of the object's name.

Wrapping Up

Now you should know the basic uses for the doctest module. You can write self-testing docstrings with this knowledge as now the docstrings not only document your code, but they also allow you to test it. If you find yourself needing to write more in-depth documentation, then you can actually write it in a simple mark-up language known as ReStructuredText, which is what the official Python documentation itself is written in. Then you can run doctest against your documentation files and make sure you haven't broken your code when you inevitably need to update it. The doctest module really is a handy little tool to keep at hand.

https://docs.python.org/3/library/doctest.html https://pymotw.com/2/doctest/ http://www.blog.pythonlibrary.org/2014/03/17/python-testing-with-doctest/

Chapter 24 - The unittest Module

The **unittest** module is actually a testing framework that was originally inspired by JUnit. It currently supports test automation, the sharing of setup and shutdown code, aggregating tests into collections and the independence of tests from the reporting framework.

The unittest frameworks supports the following concepts:

- Test Fixture - A fixture is what is used to setup a test so it can be run and also tears down when the test is finished. For example, you might need to create a temporary database before the test can be run and destroy it once the test finishes.
- Test Case - The test case is your actual test. It will typically check (or assert) that a specific response comes from a specific set of inputs. The unittest frameworks provides a base class called **TestCase** that you can use to create new test cases.
- Test Suite - The test suite is a collection of test cases, test suites or both.
- Test Runner - A runner is what controls or orchestrates the running of the tests or suites. It will also provide the outcome to the user (i.e. did they pass or fail). A runner can use a graphical user interface or be a simple text interface.

A Simple Example

I always find a code example or two to be the quickest way to learn how something new works. So let's create a little module that we will call **mymath.py**. Then put the following code into it:

```
1  def add(a, b):
2      return a + b
3
4
5  def subtract(a, b):
6      return a - b
7
8
9  def multiply(a, b):
10     return a * b
11
```

```
12
13  def divide(numerator, denominator):
14      return float(numerator) / denominator
```

This module defines four mathematical functions: add, subtract, multiply and divide. They do not do any error checking and they actually don't do exactly what you might expect. For example, if you were to call the **add** function with two strings, it would happily concatenate them together and return them. But for the purposes of illustration, this module will do for creating a test case. So let's actually write a test case for the add function! We will call this script **test_mymath.py** and save it in the same folder that contains **mymath.py**.

```python
1   import mymath
2   import unittest
3
4   class TestAdd(unittest.TestCase):
5       """
6       Test the add function from the mymath library
7       """
8
9       def test_add_integers(self):
10          """
11          Test that the addition of two integers returns the correct total
12          """
13          result = mymath.add(1, 2)
14          self.assertEqual(result, 3)
15
16      def test_add_floats(self):
17          """
18          Test that the addition of two floats returns the correct result
19          """
20          result = mymath.add(10.5, 2)
21          self.assertEqual(result, 12.5)
22
23      def test_add_strings(self):
24          """
25          Test the addition of two strings returns the two string as one
26          concatenated string
27          """
28          result = mymath.add('abc', 'def')
29          self.assertEqual(result, 'abcdef')
30
31
```

```
32  if __name__ == '__main__':
33      unittest.main()
```

Let's take a moment and go over how this code works. First we import our mymath module and Python's **unittest** module. Then we subclass **TestCase** and add three tests, which translates into three methods. The first function tests the addition of two integers; the second function tests the addition of two floating point numbers; and the last function concatenates two strings together. Finally we call unittest's **main** method at the end.

You will note that each method begins with the letters "test". This is actually important! It tells the test runner which methods are tests that it should run. Each test should have at least one assert which will verify that the result is as we expected. The unittest module supports many different types of asserts. You can test for exceptions, for Boolean conditions, and for many other conditions.

Let's try running out test. Open up a terminal and navigate to the folder that contains your mymath module and your test module:

```
1  python test_mymath.py
```

This will execute our test and we should get the following output:

```
1  ...
2  ----------------------------------------------------------------------
3  Ran 3 tests in 0.001s
4
5  OK
```

You will note that there are three periods. Each period represents a test that has passed. Then it tells us that it ran 3 tests, the time it took and the result: OK. That tells us that all the tests passed successfully.

You can make the output a bit more verbose by passing in the -**v** flag:

```
1  python test_mymath.py -v
```

This will cause the following output to be printed to stdout:

```
1   test_add_floats (__main__.TestAdd) ... ok
2   test_add_integers (__main__.TestAdd) ... ok
3   test_add_strings (__main__.TestAdd) ... ok
4
5   ----------------------------------------------------------------
6   Ran 3 tests in 0.000s
7
8   OK
```

As you can see, this shows us exactly what tests were run and the results of each test. This also leads us into our next section where we will learn about some of the commands we can use with unittest on the command line.

Command-Line Interface

The unittest module comes with a few other commands that you might find useful. To find out what they are, you can run the unittest module directly and pass it the **-h** as shown below:

```
1   python -m unittest -h
```

This will cause the following output to be printed to stdout. Note that I have cut out a portion of the output that covered **Test Discovery** command line options for brevity:

```
1   usage: python -m unittest [-h] [-v] [-q] [--locals] [-f] [-c] [-b]
2                             [tests [tests ...]]
3
4   positional arguments:
5     tests            a list of any number of test modules, classes and test
6                      methods.
7
8   optional arguments:
9     -h, --help       show this help message and exit
10    -v, --verbose    Verbose output
11    -q, --quiet      Quiet output
12    --locals         Show local variables in tracebacks
13    -f, --failfast   Stop on first fail or error
14    -c, --catch      Catch ctrl-C and display results so far
15    -b, --buffer     Buffer stdout and stderr during tests
16
17  Examples:
18    python -m unittest test_module               - run tests from test_module
19    python -m unittest module.TestClass          - run tests from module.TestClass
20    python -m unittest module.Class.test_method  - run specified test method
```

Now we have some ideas of how we might call our test code if it didn't have the call to **unittest.main()** at the bottom. In fact, go ahead and re-save that code with a different name, such as **test_mymath2.py** with the last two lines removed. Then run the following command:

```
1  python -m unittest test_mymath2.py
```

This should result in the same output we got previously:

```
1  . . .
2  ----------------------------------------------------------------------
3  Ran 3 tests in 0.000s
4
5  OK
```

The cool thing about using the unittest module on the command line is that we can use it to call specific functions in our test. Here's an example:

```
1  python -m unittest test_mymath2.TestAdd.test_add_integers
```

This command will run only run test, so the output from this command should look like this:

```
1  .
2  ----------------------------------------------------------------------
3  Ran 1 test in 0.000s
4
5  OK
```

Alternatively, if you had multiple test cases in this test module, then you could call just one test case at a time, like this:

```
1  python -m unittest test_mymath2.TestAdd
```

All this does is call our **TestAdd** subclass and runs all the test methods in it. So the result should be the same as if we ran it in the first example:

```
1   ...
2   ------------------------------------------------------------------
3   Ran 3 tests in 0.000s
4
5   OK
```

The point of this exercise is that if you were to have additional test cases in this test module, then this method gives you a method to run individual test cases instead of all of them.

Creating a More Complex Test

Most code is a lot more complex than our **mymath.py** example. So let's create a piece of code that depends on a database being in existence. We will create a simple script that can create the database with some initial data if it doesn't exist along with a few functions that will allow us to query it, delete and update rows. We will name this script **simple_db.py**. This is a fairly long example, so bear with me:

```python
import sqlite3

def create_database():
    conn = sqlite3.connect("mydatabase.db")
    cursor = conn.cursor()

    # create a table
    cursor.execute("""CREATE TABLE albums
                          (title text, artist text, release_date text,
                           publisher text, media_type text)
                       """)
    # insert some data
    cursor.execute("INSERT INTO albums VALUES "
                   "('Glow', 'Andy Hunter', '7/24/2012',"
                   "'Xplore Records', 'MP3')")

    # save data to database
    conn.commit()

    # insert multiple records using the more secure "?" method
    albums = [('Exodus', 'Andy Hunter', '7/9/2002',
               'Sparrow Records', 'CD'),
              ('Until We Have Faces', 'Red', '2/1/2011',
               'Essential Records', 'CD'),
```

```
25                      ('The End is Where We Begin', 'Thousand Foot Krutch',
26                       '4/17/2012', 'TFKmusic', 'CD'),
27                      ('The Good Life', 'Trip Lee', '4/10/2012',
28                       'Reach Records', 'CD')]
29       cursor.executemany("INSERT INTO albums VALUES (?,?,?,?,?)",
30                           albums)
31       conn.commit()
32
33   def delete_artist(artist):
34       """
35       Delete an artist from the database
36       """
37       conn = sqlite3.connect("mydatabase.db")
38       cursor = conn.cursor()
39
40       sql = """
41       DELETE FROM albums
42       WHERE artist = ?
43       """
44       cursor.execute(sql, [(artist)])
45       conn.commit()
46       cursor.close()
47       conn.close()
48
49
50   def update_artist(artist, new_name):
51       """
52       Update the artist name
53       """
54       conn = sqlite3.connect("mydatabase.db")
55       cursor = conn.cursor()
56
57       sql = """
58       UPDATE albums
59       SET artist = ?
60       WHERE artist = ?
61       """
62       cursor.execute(sql, (new_name, artist))
63       conn.commit()
64       cursor.close()
65       conn.close()
66
```

```python
67
68   def select_all_albums(artist):
69       """
70       Query the database for all the albums by a particular artist
71       """
72       conn = sqlite3.connect("mydatabase.db")
73       cursor = conn.cursor()
74
75       sql = "SELECT * FROM albums WHERE artist=?"
76       cursor.execute(sql, [(artist)])
77       result = cursor.fetchall()
78       cursor.close()
79       conn.close()
80       return result
81
82
83   if __name__ == '__main__':
84       import os
85       if not os.path.exists("mydatabase.db"):
86           create_database()
87
88       delete_artist('Andy Hunter')
89       update_artist('Red', 'Redder')
90       print(select_all_albums('Thousand Foot Krutch'))
```

You can play around with this code a bit to see how it works. Once you're comfortable with it, then we can move on to testing it.

Now some might argue that creating a database and destroying it for each test is pretty big overhead. And they might have a good point. However, to test certain functionality, you sometimes need to do this sort of thing. Besides, you don't usually need to create the entire production database just for sanity checks.

Anyway, this is once again for illustrative purposes. The unittest module allows us to override **setUp** and **tearDown** methods for these types of things. So we will create a setUp method that will create the database and a tearDown method that will delete it when the test is over. Note that the setup and tear down will occur for each test. This prevents the tests from altering the database in such a way that a subsequent test will fail.

Let's take a look at the first part of the test case class. Save the following code in a file named *test_db.py*:

```python
1   import os
2   import simple_db
3   import sqlite3
4   import unittest
5
6   class TestMusicDatabase(unittest.TestCase):
7       """
8       Test the music database
9       """
10
11      def setUp(self):
12          """
13          Setup a temporary database
14          """
15          conn = sqlite3.connect("mydatabase.db")
16          cursor = conn.cursor()
17
18          # create a table
19          cursor.execute("""CREATE TABLE albums
20                            (title text, artist text, release_date text,
21                             publisher text, media_type text)
22                         """)
23          # insert some data
24          cursor.execute("INSERT INTO albums VALUES "
25                         "('Glow', 'Andy Hunter', '7/24/2012',"
26                         "'Xplore Records', 'MP3')")
27
28          # save data to database
29          conn.commit()
30
31          # insert multiple records using the more secure "?" method
32          albums = [('Exodus', 'Andy Hunter', '7/9/2002',
33                     'Sparrow Records', 'CD'),
34                    ('Until We Have Faces', 'Red', '2/1/2011',
35                     'Essential Records', 'CD'),
36                    ('The End is Where We Begin', 'Thousand Foot Krutch',
37                     '4/17/2012', 'TFKmusic', 'CD'),
38                    ('The Good Life', 'Trip Lee', '4/10/2012',
39                     'Reach Records', 'CD')]
40          cursor.executemany("INSERT INTO albums VALUES (?,?,?,?,?)",
41                             albums)
42          conn.commit()
```

```
43
44    def tearDown(self):
45        """
46        Delete the database
47        """
48        os.remove("mydatabase.db")
```

The **setUp** method will create our database and then populate it with some data. The **tearDown** method will delete our database file. If you were using something like MySQL or Microsoft SQL Server for your database, then you would probably just drop the table, but with sqlite, we can just delete the whole thing.

Now let's add a couple of actual tests to our code. You can just add these to the end of the test class above:

```
1    def test_updating_artist(self):
2        """
3        Tests that we can successfully update an artist's name
4        """
5        simple_db.update_artist('Red', 'Redder')
6        actual = simple_db.select_all_albums('Redder')
7        expected = [('Until We Have Faces', 'Redder',
8                     '2/1/2011', 'Essential Records', 'CD')]
9        self.assertListEqual(expected, actual)
10
11   def test_artist_does_not_exist(self):
12       """
13       Test that an artist does not exist
14       """
15       result = simple_db.select_all_albums('Redder')
16       self.assertFalse(result)
```

The first test will update the name of one of the artists to the string **Redder**. Then we do a query to make sure that the new artist name exists. The next test will also check to see if the artist known as "Redder" exists. This time it shouldn't as the database was deleted and recreated between tests. Let's try running it to see what happens:

```
1    python -m unittest test_db.py
```

The command above should result in the output below, although your runtime will probably differ:

```
1   ..
2   ---------------------------------------------------------------------
3   Ran 2 tests in 0.032s
4
5   OK
```

Pretty cool, eh? Now we can move on to learn about test suites!

Creating Test Suites

As was mentioned at the beginning, a test suite is just a collection of test cases, test suites or both. Most of the time, when you call **unittest.main()**, it will do the right thing and gather all the module's test cases for you before executing them. But sometimes you will want to be the one in control. In that circumstance, you can use the **TestSuite** class. Here's an example of how you might use it:

```
1   import unittest
2
3   from test_mymath import TestAdd
4
5
6   def my_suite():
7       suite = unittest.TestSuite()
8       result = unittest.TestResult()
9       suite.addTest(unittest.makeSuite(TestAdd))
10      runner = unittest.TextTestRunner()
11      print(runner.run(suite))
12
13  my_suite()
```

Creating your own suite is a slightly convoluted process. First you need to create an instance of **TestSuite** and an instance of **TestResult**. The TestResult class just holds the results of the tests. Next we call **addTest** on our suite object. This is where it gets a bit weird. If you just pass in **TestAdd**, then it has to be an instance of TestAdd and TestAdd must also implement a **runTest** method. Since we didn't do that, we use unittest's **makeSuite** function to turn our TestCase class into a suite.

The last step is to actually run the suite, which means that we need a runner if we want nice output. Thus, we create an instance of **TextTestRunner** and have it run our suite. If you do that and you print out what it returns, you should get something like this printed out to your screen:

```
1   ...
2   ----------------------------------------------------------------
3   Ran 3 tests in 0.001s
4
5   OK
6   <unittest.runner.TextTestResult run=3 errors=0 failures=0>
```

An alternative is to just call **suite.run(result)** and print out its result. However all that will give you is a TestResult object that looks very similar to that last line of output above. If you want the more usual output, then you will want to use a runner.

How to Skip Tests

The unittest module supports skipping tests as of Python 3.1. There are a few use cases for skipping tests:

- You might want to skip a test if the version of a library doesn't support what you want to test
- The test is dependent on the operating system it is running under
- Or you have some other criteria for skipping a test

Let's change our test case so it has a couple of tests that will be skipped:

```python
1   import mymath
2   import sys
3   import unittest
4
5   class TestAdd(unittest.TestCase):
6       """
7       Test the add function from the mymath module
8       """
9
10      def test_add_integers(self):
11          """
12          Test that the addition of two integers returns the correct total
13          """
14          result = mymath.add(1, 2)
15          self.assertEqual(result, 3)
16
17      def test_add_floats(self):
18          """
```

```
19              Test that the addition of two floats returns the correct result
20              """
21          result = mymath.add(10.5, 2)
22          self.assertEqual(result, 12.5)
23
24      @unittest.skip('Skip this test')
25      def test_add_strings(self):
26              """
27              Test the addition of two strings returns the two string as one
28              concatenated string
29              """
30          result = mymath.add('abc', 'def')
31          self.assertEqual(result, 'abcdef')
32
33      @unittest.skipUnless(sys.platform.startswith("win"), "requires Windows")
34      def test_adding_on_windows(self):
35          result = mymath.add(1, 2)
36          self.assertEqual(result, 3)
```

Here we demonstrate two different methods of skipping a test: **skip** and **skipUnless**. You will notice that we are decorating the functions that need to be skipped. The **skip** decorator can be used to skip any test for any reason. The **skipUnless** decorator will skip a test unless the condition returns True. So if you run this test on Mac or Linux, it will get skipped. There is also a **skipIf** decorator that will skip a test if the condition is True.

You can run this script with the verbose flag to see why it's skipping tests:

```
1  python -m unittest test_mymath.py -v
```

This command will result in the following output:

```
1  test_add_floats (test_mymath4.TestAdd) ... ok
2  test_add_integers (test_mymath4.TestAdd) ... ok
3  test_add_strings (test_mymath4.TestAdd) ... skipped 'Skip this test'
4  test_adding_on_windows (test_mymath4.TestAdd) ... skipped 'requires Windows'
5
6  ----------------------------------------------------------------------
7  Ran 4 tests in 0.000s
8
9  OK (skipped=2)
```

This output tells us that we attempted to run four tests, but skipped two of them.

There is also an **expectedFailure** decorator that you can add to a test that you know will fail. I'll leave that one for you to try out on your own.

Integrating with doctest

The unittest module can be used with Python's doctest module as well. If you have created a lot of modules that have doctests in them, you will usually want to be able to run them systematically. This is where unittest comes in. The unittest module supports **Test Discovery** starting in Python 3.2. Test Discovery basically allows unittest to look at a the contents of a directory and determine from the file name which ones might contain tests. It then loads the test by importing them.

Let's create a new empty folder and inside of it, we will create a file called **my_docs.py**. It will need to have the following code:

```
1   def add(a, b):
2       """
3       Return the addition of the arguments: a + b
4
5       >>> add(1, 2)
6       3
7       >>> add(-1, 10)
8       9
9       >>> add('a', 'b')
10      'ab'
11      >>> add(1, '2')
12      Traceback (most recent call last):
13        File "test.py", line 17, in <module>
14          add(1, '2')
15        File "test.py", line 14, in add
16          return a + b
17      TypeError: unsupported operand type(s) for +: 'int' and 'str'
18      """
19      return a + b
20
21  def subtract(a, b):
22      """
23      Returns the result of subtracting b from a
24
25      >>> subtract(2, 1)
26      1
27      >>> subtract(10, 10)
28      0
29      >>> subtract(7, 10)
30      -3
31      """
32      return a - b
```

Now we need to to create another module in the same location as this one that will turn our doctests into unittests. Let's call this file **test_doctests.py**. Put the following code inside of it:

```
1  import doctest
2  import my_docs
3  import unittest
4
5  def load_tests(loader, tests, ignore):
6      tests.addTests(doctest.DocTestSuite(my_docs))
7      return tests
```

The function name is actually required here for Test Discovery to work, according to the documentation for the doctest module. What we're doing here is adding a suite to the **tests** object in much the same way as we did earlier. In this case, we are using doctest's **DocTestSuite** class. You can give this class a setUp and tearDown method as parameters should your tests need them. To run this code, you will need to execute the following command in your new folder:

```
1  python -m unittest discover
```

On my machine, I received the following output:

```
1  ..
2  ----------------------------------------------------------------
3  Ran 2 tests in 0.002s
4
5  OK
```

You will note that when you use unittest to run doctest, each docstring is considered a single test. If you were to run the docstrings with doctest directly, then you will notice that doctest will say there are more tests. Other than that, it works pretty much as expected.

Wrapping Up

We covered a lot in this chapter. You learned the basics of using the unittest module. Then we moved on and learned how to use unittest from the command line. We also found out how to set up and tear down tests. You discovered how to create test suites too. Finally we learned how to turn a series of doctests into unittests. Be sure to spend some time reading the documentation on both of these fine libraries as there is a lot of additional functionality that was not covered here.

Chapter 25 - The mock Module

The unittest module now includes a **mock** submodule as of Python 3.3. It will allow you to replace portions of the system that you are testing with mock objects as well as make assertions about how they were used. A mock object is used for simulating system resources that aren't available in your test environment. In other words, you will find times when you want to test some part of your code in isolation from the rest of it or you will need to test some code in isolation from outside services.

Note that if you have a version of Python prior to Python 3, you can download the Mock library and get the same functionality.

Let's think about why you might want to use mock. One good example is if your application is tied to some kind of third party service, such as Twitter or Facebook. If your application's test suite goes out and retweets a bunch of items or "likes" a bunch of posts every time its run, then that is probably undesirable behavior since it will be doing that every time the test is run. Another example might be if you had designed a tool for making updates to your database tables easier. Each time the test runs, it will do some updates on the same records every time and could wipe out valuable data.

Instead of doing any of those things, you can use unittest's mock. It will allow you to mock and stub out those kinds of side-effects so you don't have to worry about them. Instead of interacting with the third party resources, you will be running your test against a dummy API that matches those resources. The piece that you care about the most is that your application is calling the functions it's supposed to. You probably don't care as much if the API itself actually executes. Of course, there are times when you will want to do an end-to-end test that does actually execute the API, but those tests don't need mocks!

Simple Examples

The Python mock class can mimic and other Python class. This allows you to examine what methods were called on your mocked class and even what parameters were passed to them. Let's start by looking at a couple of simple examples that demonstrate how to use the mock module:

```
1  >>> from unittest.mock import Mock
2  >>> my_mock = Mock()
3  >>> my_mock.__str__ = Mock(return_value='Mocking')
4  >>> str(my_mock)
5  'Mocking'
```

In this example, we import **Mock** class from the **unittest.mock** module. Then we create an instance of the Mock class. Finally we set our mock object's **__str__** method, which is the magic method that controls what happens if you call Python's **str** function on an object. In this case, we just return the string "Mocking", which is what you see when we actually execute the str() function at the end.

The mock module also supports five asserts. Let's take a look at how at a couple of those in action:

```
1  >>> from unittest.mock import Mock
2  >>> class TestClass():
3  ...      pass
4  ...
5  >>> cls = TestClass()
6  >>> cls.method = Mock(return_value='mocking is fun')
7  >>> cls.method(1, 2, 3)
8  'mocking is fun'
9  >>> cls.method.assert_called_once_with(1, 2, 3)
10 >>> cls.method(1, 2, 3)
11 'mocking is fun'
12 >>> cls.method.assert_called_once_with(1, 2, 3)
13 Traceback (most recent call last):
14   Python Shell, prompt 9, line 1
15   File "/usr/local/lib/python3.5/unittest/mock.py", line 802, in assert_called_o\
16 nce_with
17     raise AssertionError(msg)
18 builtins.AssertionError: Expected 'mock' to be called once. Called 2 times.
19 >>> cls.other_method = Mock(return_value='Something else')
20 >>> cls.other_method.assert_not_called()
```

First off, we do our import and create an empty class. Then we create an instance of the class and add a method that returns a string using the Mock class. Then we call the method with three integers are arguments. As you will note, this returned the string that we set earlier as the return value. Now we can test out an assert! So we call the **assert_called_once_with** assert which will assert if we call our method two or more times with the same arguments. The first time we call the assert, it passes. So then we call the method again with the same methods and run the assert a second time to see what happens.

As you can see, we got an **AssertionError**. To round out the example, we go ahead and create a second method that we don't call at all and then assert that it wasn't called via the **assert_not_called** assert.

Side Effects

You can also create side effects of mock objects via the **side_effect** argument. A side effect is something that happens when you run your function. For example, some videogames have integration into social media. When you score a certain number of points, win a trophy, complete a level or some other predetermined goal, it will record it AND also post about it to Twitter, Facebook or whatever it is integrated with. Another side effect to running a function is that it might be tied to closely with your user interface and cause it to redraw unnecessarily.

Since we know about these kinds of side effect up front, we can mock them in our code. Let's look at a simple example:

```
1  from unittest.mock import Mock
2
3
4  def my_side_effect():
5      print('Updating database!')
6
7  def main():
8      mock = Mock(side_effect=my_side_effect)
9      mock()
10
11 if __name__ == '__main__':
12     main()
```

Here we create a function that pretends to update a database. Then in our **main** function, we create a mock object and give it a side effect. Finally we call our mock object. If you do this, you should see a message printed to stdout about the database being updated.

The Python documentation also points out that you can make side effect raise an exception if you want to. One fairly common reason to want to raise an exception if you called it incorrectly. An example might be that you didn't pass in enough arguments. You could also create a mock that raises a Deprecation warning.

Autospeccing

The mock module also supports the concept of **auto-speccing**. The autospec allows you to create mock objects that contain the same attributes and methods of the objects that you are replacing with your mock. They will even have the same call signature as the real object! You can create an autospec with the **create_autospec** function or by passing in the **autospec** argument to the mock library's **patch** decorator, which we'll be looking at in the next section.

For now, let's look at an easy-to-understand example of the autospec:

```
1   >>> from unittest.mock import create_autospec
2   >>> def add(a, b):
3   ...        return a + b
4   ...
5   >>> mocked_func = create_autospec(add, return_value=10)
6   >>> mocked_func(1, 2)
7   10
8   >>> mocked_func(1, 2, 3)
9   Traceback (most recent call last):
10    Python Shell, prompt 5, line 1
11    File "<string>", line 2, in add
12    File "/Library/Frameworks/Python.framework/Versions/3.5/lib/python3.5/unittest\
13  /mock.py", line 181, in checksig
14      sig.bind(*args, **kwargs)
15    File "/Library/Frameworks/Python.framework/Versions/3.5/lib/python3.5/inspect.\
16  py", line 2921, in bind
17      return args[0]._bind(args[1:], kwargs)
18    File "/Library/Frameworks/Python.framework/Versions/3.5/lib/python3.5/inspect.\
19  py", line 2842, in _bind
20      raise TypeError('too many positional arguments') from None
21  builtins.TypeError: too many positional arguments
```

In this example, we import the **create_autospec** function and then create a simple adding function. Next we use create_autospec() by passing it our **add** function and setting its return value to 10. As long as you pass this new mocked version of add with two arguments, it will always return 10. However, if you call it with the incorrect number of arguments, you will receive an exception.

The Patch

The mock module has a neat little function called **patch** that can be used as a function decorator, a class decorator or even a context manager. This will allow you to easily create mock classes or objects in a module that you want to test as it will be replaced by a mock.

Let's start out by creating a simple function for reading web pages. We will call it **webreader.py**. Here's the code:

```
1   import urllib.request
2
3   def read_webpage(url):
4       response = urllib.request.urlopen(url)
5       return response.read()
```

This code is pretty self-explanatory. All it does is take a URL, opens the page, reads the HTML and returns it. Now in our test environment we don't want to get bogged down reading data from websites especially is our application happens to be a web crawler that downloads gigabytes worth of data every day. Instead, we want to create a mocked version of Python's urllib so that we can call our function above without actually downloading anything.

Let's create a file named **mock_webreader.py** and save it in the same location as the code above. Then put the following code into it:

```python
import webreader

from unittest.mock import patch


@patch('urllib.request.urlopen')
def dummy_reader(mock_obj):
    result = webreader.read_webpage('https://www.google.com/')
    mock_obj.assert_called_with('https://www.google.com/')
    print(result)

if __name__ == '__main__':
    dummy_reader()
```

Here we just import our previously created module and the **patch** function from the mock module. Then we create a decorator that patches **urllib.request.urlopen**. Inside the function, we call our webreader module's **read_webpage** function with Google's URL and print the result. If you run this code, you will see that instead of getting HTML for our result, we get a MagicMock object instead. This demonstrates the power of patch. We can now prevent the downloading of data while still calling the original function correctly.

The documentation points out that you can stack path decorators just as you can with regular decorators. So if you have a really complex function that accesses databases or writes file or pretty much anything else, you can add multiple patches to prevent side effects from happening.

Wrapping Up

The mock module is quite useful and very powerful. It also takes some time to learn how to use properly and effectively. There are lots of examples in the Python documentation although they are all simple examples with dummy classes. I think you will find this module useful for creating robust tests that can run quickly without having unintentional side effects.

Chapter 26 - An Intro to coverage.py

Coverage.py is a 3rd party tool for Python that is used for measuring your code coverage. It was originally created by Ned Batchelder. The term "coverage" in programming circles is typically used to describe the effectiveness of your tests and how much of your code is actually covered by tests. You can use coverage.py with Python 2.6 up to the current version of Python 3 as well as with PyPy.

If you don't have coverage.py installed, you may do so using pip:

```
1  pip install coverage
```

Now that we have coverage.py installed, we need some code to use it with. Let's use the **mymath** module that we created earlier in the book. Here's the code:

```
1   def add(a, b):
2       return a + b
3
4
5   def subtract(a, b):
6       return a - b
7
8
9   def multiply(a, b):
10      return a * b
11
12
13  def divide(numerator, denominator):
14      return float(numerator) / denominator
```

Now we need a test. Fortunately we wrote a simple test in the unit testing chapter. To refresh your memory, here is the code for test:

```
1   # test_mymath.py
2   import mymath
3   import unittest
4
5   class TestAdd(unittest.TestCase):
6       """
7       Test the add function from the mymath library
8       """
9
10      def test_add_integers(self):
11          """
12          Test that the addition of two integers returns the correct total
13          """
14          result = mymath.add(1, 2)
15          self.assertEqual(result, 3)
16
17      def test_add_floats(self):
18          """
19          Test that the addition of two floats returns the correct result
20          """
21          result = mymath.add(10.5, 2)
22          self.assertEqual(result, 12.5)
23
24      def test_add_strings(self):
25          """
26          Test the addition of two strings returns the two string as one
27          concatenated string
28          """
29          result = mymath.add('abc', 'def')
30          self.assertEqual(result, 'abcdef')
31
32
33  if __name__ == '__main__':
34      unittest.main()
```

Now that we have all the pieces, we can run coverage.py using the test. Open up a terminal and navigate to the folder that contains the **mymath** module and the test code we wrote. Now we can call coverage.py like this:

```
1   coverage run test_mymath.py
```

Note that we need to call **run** to get coverage.py to run the module. If your module accepts arguments, you can pass those in as you normally would. When you do this, you will see the test's output as if you ran it yourself. You will also find a new file in the directory that is called **.coverage**. To get information out of this file, you will need to run the following command:

```
1  coverage report -m
```

Executing this command will result in the following output:

```
1  Name              Stmts   Miss  Cover   Missing
2  ------------------------------------------------
3  mymath.py             9      3    67%   9, 13, 17
4  test_mymath.py       14      0   100%
5  ------------------------------------------------
6  TOTAL                23      3    87%
```

The **-m** flag tells coverage.py that you want it to include the **Missing** column in the output. If you omit the **-m**, then you'll only get the first four columns. What you see here is that coverage ran the test code and determined that I have only 67% of the mymath module covered by my unit test. The "Missing" column tells me what lines of code still need coverage. If you look at the lines coverage.py points out, you will quickly see that my test code doesn't test the **subtract**, **multiply** or **divide** functions.

Before we try to add more test coverage, let's learn how to make coverage.py produce an HTML report. To do this, all you need to do is run the following command:

```
1  coverage html
```

This command will create a folder named **htmlcov** that contains various files. Navigate into that folder and try opening **index.html** in your browser of choice. On my machine, it loaded a page like this:

Coverage report: 87%

Module	statements	missing	excluded	coverage
mymath.py	9	3	0	67%
test_mymath.py	14	0	0	100%
Total	**23**	**3**	**0**	**87%**

coverage.py v4.1, created at 2016-07-18 15:04

You can actually click on the modules listed to load up an annotated web page that shows you what parts of the code are not covered. Since the **mymath.py** module obviously isn't covered very well, let's click on that one. You should end up seeing something like the following:

Coverage for **mymath.py** : 67%

9 statements	6 run	3 missing	0 excluded

```python
1   import argparse
2
3
4   def add(a, b):
5       return a + b
6
7
8   def subtract(a, b):
9       return a - b
10
11
12  def multiply(a, b):
13      return a * b
14
15
16  def divide(numerator, denominator):
17      return float(numerator) / denominator
```

« index   coverage.py v4.1, created at 2016-07-18 15:04

This screenshot clearly shows what parts of the code were not covered in our original unit test. Now that we know definitively what's missing in our test coverage, let's add a unit test for our **subtract** function and see how that changes things!

Open up your copy of **test_mymath.py** and add the following class to it:

```
1  class TestSubtract(unittest.TestCase):
2      """
3      Test the subtract function from the mymath library
4      """
5
6      def test_subtract_integers(self):
7          """
8          Test that subtracting integers returns the correct result
9          """
10         result = mymath.subtract(10, 8)
11         self.assertEqual(result, 2)
```

Now we need to re-run coverage against the updated test. All you need to do is re-run this command: **coverage run test_mymath.py**. The output will show that four tests have passed successfully. Now re-run **coverage html** and re-open the "index.html" file. You should now see the that we're at 78% coverage:

Coverage report: 93%

Module	statements	missing	excluded	coverage
mymath.py	9	2	0	78%
test_mymath.py	18	0	0	100%
Total	**27**	**2**	**0**	**93%**

coverage.py v4.1, created at 2016-07-18 16:08

This is an 11% improvement! Let's go ahead and add a simple test for the multiply and divide functions and see if we can hit 100% coverage!

```
1  class TestMultiply(unittest.TestCase):
2      """
3      Test the multiply function from the mymath library
4      """
5
6      def test_subtract_integers(self):
7          """
8          Test that multiplying integers returns the correct result
9          """
```

```
10        result = mymath.multiply(5, 50)
11        self.assertEqual(result, 250)
12
13
14 class TestDivide(unittest.TestCase):
15     """
16     Test the divide function from the mymath library
17     """
18
19     def test_divide_by_zero(self):
20         """
21         Test that multiplying integers returns the correct result
22         """
23         with self.assertRaises(ZeroDivisionError):
24             result = mymath.divide(8, 0)
```

Now you can re-run the same commands as before and reload the "index.html" file. When you do, you should see something like the following:

Coverage report: 100%

Module	statements	missing	excluded	coverage
mymath.py	9	0	0	100%
test_mymath.py	26	0	0	100%
Total	**35**	**0**	**0**	**100%**

coverage.py v4.1, created at 2016-07-18 16:20

As you can see, we have hit full test coverage! Of course, full coverage in this case means that each function is exercised by our test suite. The problem with this is that we have three times the number of tests for the addition function versus the others, but coverage.py doesn't give us any kind of data about that. However it will give us a good idea of basic coverage even if it can't tell us if we've tested every possible argument permutation imaginable.

Additional Information

I just wanted to mention a few other features of coverage.py without going into a lot of detail. First, coverage.py supports configuration files. The configuration file format is your classic ".ini" file with sections demarcated by the fact that they are surrounded with square braces (i.e. [my_section]). You can add comments to the config file using the following # or ; (semi-colon).

Coverage.py also allows you to specify what source files you want it to analyze via the configuration file we mentioned previously. Once you have the configuration set up the way you want it, then you can run coverage.py. It also supports a "–source" command-line switch. Finally you can use the "–include" and "–omit" switches to include a list of file name patterns or exclude them. These switches have matching configuration values that you can add to your configuration file too.

The last item that I want to mention is that coverage.py supports plugins. You can write your own or download and install someone else's plugin to enhance coverage.py.

Wrapping Up

You now know the basics of coverage.py and what this special package is useful for. Coverage.py allows you to check your tests and find holes in your test coverage. If you aren't sure you've got your code tested properly, this package will help you ascertain where the holes are if they exist. Of course, you are still responsible for writing good tests. If your tests aren't valid but they pass anyway, coverage.py won't help you.

Part V - Concurrency

Python includes several modules to help you write concurrent code. In case you're wondering, the idea behind concurrent code is that it allows you to do more then one task at the same time. For example, in regular Python code, if you wanted to download a list of files from the Internet, you would iterate over the list and download each one in a serial manner (i.e. one at a time). With concurrency, you can start multiple files downloading at the same time and potentially speed up the process.

We will be looking at the following modules in this section:

- Chapter 27 - The asyncio module
- Chapter 28 - The threading module
- Chapter 29 - The multiprocessing module
- Chapter 30 - The concurrent.futures module

These modules will help you write useful and efficient code that you can use in your current and future projects.

Let's get started!

Chapter 27 - The asyncio Module

The **asyncio** module was added to Python in version 3.4 as a provisional package. What that means is that it is possible that asyncio receives backwards incompatible changes or could even be removed in a future release of Python. According to the documentation asyncio *"provides infrastructure for writing single-threaded concurrent code using coroutines, multiplexing I/O access over sockets and other resources, running network clients and servers, and other related primitives"*. This chapter is not meant to cover everything you can do with asyncio, however you will learn how to use the module and why it is useful.

If you need something like asyncio in an older version of Python, then you might want to take a look at Twisted or gevent.

Definitions

The asyncio module provides a framework that revolves around the *event loop*. An event loop basically waits for something to happen and then acts on the event. It is responsible for handling such things as I/O and system events. Asyncio actually has several loop implementations available to it. The module will default to the one most likely to be the most efficient for the operating system it is running under; however you can explicitly choose the event loop if you so desire. An event loop basically says "when event A happens, react with function B".

Think of a server as it waits for someone to come along and ask for a resource, such as a web page. If the website isn't very popular, the server will be idle for a long time. But when it does get a hit, then the server needs to react. This reaction is known as event handling. When a user loads the web page, the server will check for and call one or more event handlers. Once those event handlers are done, they need to give control back to the event loop. To do this in Python, asyncio uses *coroutines*.

A coroutine is a special function that can give up control to its caller without losing its state. A coroutine is a consumer and an extension of a generator. One of their big benefits over threads is that they don't use very much memory to execute. Note that when you call a coroutine function, it doesn't actually execute. Instead it will return a coroutine object that you can pass to the event loop to have it executed either immediately or later on.

One other term you will likely run across when you are using the asyncio module is *future*. A *future* is basically an object that represents the result of work that hasn't completed. Your event loop can watch future objects and wait for them to finish. When a future finishes, it is set to done. Asyncio also supports locks and semaphores.

The last piece of information I want to mention is the *Task*. A Task is a wrapper for a coroutine and a subclass of Future. You can even schedule a Task using the event loop.

async and await

The **async** and **await** keywords were added in Python 3.5 to define a **native coroutine** and make them a distinct type when compared with a generator based coroutine. If you'd like an in-depth description of async and await, you will want to check out PEP 492.

In Python 3.4, you would create a coroutine like this:

```
1   # Python 3.4 coroutine example
2   import asyncio
3
4   @asyncio.coroutine
5   def my_coro():
6       yield from func()
```

This decorator still works in Python 3.5, but the **types** module received an update in the form of a **coroutine** function which will now tell you if what you're interacting with is a native coroutine or not. Starting in Python 3.5, you can use async def to syntactically define a coroutine function. So the function above would end up looking like this:

```
1   import asyncio
2
3   async def my_coro():
4       await func()
```

When you define a coroutine in this manner, you cannot use **yield** inside the coroutine function. Instead it must include a **return** or **await** statement that are used for returning values to the caller. Note that the **await** keyword can only be used inside an **async def** function.

The **async** / **await** keywords can be considered an API to be used for asynchronous programming. The asyncio module is just a framework that happens to use **async** / **await** for programming asynchronously. There is actually a project called **curio** that proves this concept as it is a separate implementation of an event loop thats uses **async** / **await** underneath the covers.

A Coroutine Example

While it is certainly helpful to have a lot of background information into how all this works, sometimes you just want to see some examples so you can get a feel for the syntax and how to put things together. So with that in mind, let's start out with a simple example!

A fairly common task that you will want to complete is downloading a file from some location whether that be an internal resource or a file on the Internet. Usually you will want to download more than one file. So let's create a pair of coroutines that can do that:

```python
1   import asyncio
2   import os
3   import urllib.request
4
5   async def download_coroutine(url):
6       """
7       A coroutine to download the specified url
8       """
9       request = urllib.request.urlopen(url)
10      filename = os.path.basename(url)
11
12      with open(filename, 'wb') as file_handle:
13          while True:
14              chunk = request.read(1024)
15              if not chunk:
16                  break
17              file_handle.write(chunk)
18      msg = 'Finished downloading {filename}'.format(filename=filename)
19      return msg
20
21  async def main(urls):
22      """
23      Creates a group of coroutines and waits for them to finish
24      """
25      coroutines = [download_coroutine(url) for url in urls]
26      completed, pending = await asyncio.wait(coroutines)
27      for item in completed:
28          print(item.result())
29
30
31  if __name__ == '__main__':
32      urls = ["http://www.irs.gov/pub/irs-pdf/f1040.pdf",
33              "http://www.irs.gov/pub/irs-pdf/f1040a.pdf",
```

```
34                    "http://www.irs.gov/pub/irs-pdf/f1040ez.pdf",
35                    "http://www.irs.gov/pub/irs-pdf/f1040es.pdf",
36                    "http://www.irs.gov/pub/irs-pdf/f1040sb.pdf"]
37
38        event_loop = asyncio.get_event_loop()
39        try:
40            event_loop.run_until_complete(main(urls))
41        finally:
42            event_loop.close()
```

In this code, we import the modules that we need and then create our first coroutine using the **async** syntax. This coroutine is called **download_coroutine** and it uses Python's **urllib** to download whatever URL is passed to it. When it is done, it will return a message that says so.

The other coroutine is our main coroutine. It basically takes a list of one or more URLs and queues them up. We use asyncio's **wait** function to wait for the coroutines to finish. Of course, to actually start the coroutines, they need to be added to the event loop. We do that at the very end where we get an event loop and then call its **run_until_complete** method. You will note that we pass in the **main** coroutine to the event loop. This starts running the main coroutine which queues up the second coroutine and gets it going. This is known as a chained coroutine.

Scheduling Calls

You can also schedule calls to regular functions using the asyncio event loop. The first method we'll look at is **call_soon**. The **call_soon** method will basically call your callback or event handler as soon as it can. It works as a FIFO queue, so if some of the callbacks take a while to run, then the others will be delayed until the previous ones have finished. Let's look at an example:

```
1   import asyncio
2   import functools
3
4
5   def event_handler(loop, stop=False):
6       print('Event handler called')
7       if stop:
8           print('stopping the loop')
9           loop.stop()
10
11
12  if __name__ == '__main__':
13      loop = asyncio.get_event_loop()
14      try:
```

```
15            loop.call_soon(functools.partial(event_handler, loop))
16            print('starting event loop')
17            loop.call_soon(functools.partial(event_handler, loop, stop=True))
18
19            loop.run_forever()
20        finally:
21            print('closing event loop')
22            loop.close()
```

The majority of asyncio's functions do not accept keywords, so we will need the **functools** module if we need to pass keywords to our event handler. Our regular function will print some text out to stdout whenever it is called. If you happen to set its **stop** argument to **True**, it will also stop the event loop.

The first time we call it, we do not stop the loop. The second time we call it, we do stop the loop. The reason we want to stop the loop is that we've told it to **run_forever**, which will put the event loop into an infinite loop. Once the loop is stopped, we can close it. If you run this code, you should see the following output:

```
1   starting event loop
2   Event handler called
3   Event handler called
4   stopping the loop
5   closing event loop
```

There is a related function called **call_soon_threadsafe**. As the name implies, it works the same way as **call_soon**, but it's thread-safe.

If you want to actually delay a call until some time in the future, you can do so using the **call_later** function. In this case, we could change our call_soon signature to the following:

```
1   loop.call_later(1, event_handler, loop)
```

This will delay calling our event handler for one second, then it will call it and pass the loop in as its first parameter.

If you want to schedule a specific time in the future, then you will need to grab the loop's time rather than the computer's time. You can do so like this:

```
1   current_time = loop.time()
```

Once you have that, then you can just use the **call_at** function and pass it the time that you want it to call your event handler. So let's say we want to call our event handler five minutes from now. Here's how you might do it:

```
1  loop.call_at(current_time + 300, event_handler, loop)
```

In this example, we use the current time that we grabbed and append 300 seconds or five minutes to it. By so doing, we delay calling our event handler for five minutes! Pretty neat!

Tasks

Tasks are a subclass of a Future and a wrapper around a coroutine. They give you the ability to keep track of when they finish processing. Because they are a type of Future, other coroutines can wait for a task and you can also grab the result of a task when it's done processing. Let's take a look at a simple example:

```python
1  import asyncio
2  import time
3
4  async def my_task(seconds):
5      """
6      A task to do for a number of seconds
7      """
8      print('This task is taking {} seconds to complete'.format(
9          seconds))
10     time.sleep(seconds)
11     return 'task finished'
12
13
14 if __name__ == '__main__':
15     my_event_loop = asyncio.get_event_loop()
16     try:
17         print('task creation started')
18         task_obj = my_event_loop.create_task(my_task(seconds=2))
19         my_event_loop.run_until_complete(task_obj)
20     finally:
21         my_event_loop.close()
22
23     print("The task's result was: {}".format(task_obj.result()))
```

Here we create an asynchronous function that accepts the number of seconds it will take for the function to run. This simulates a long running process. Then we create our event loop and then create a task object by calling the event loop object's **create_task** function. The **create_task** function accepts the function that we want to turn into a task. Then we tell the event loop to run until the task completes. At the very end, we get the result of the task since it has finished.

Tasks can also be canceled very easily by using their **cancel** method. Just call it when you want to end a task. Should a task get canceled when it is waiting for another operation, the task will raise a **CancelledError**.

Wrapping Up

At this point, you should know enough to start working with the asyncio library on your own. The asyncio library is very powerful and allows you to do a lot of really cool and interesting tasks. You should check out http://asyncio.org/ which is a curated listing of various projects that are using asyncio. It is a wonderful place to get ideas for how to use this library. The Python documentation is also a great place to start from.

Chapter 28 - The threading Module

The **threading** module was first introduced in Python 1.5.2 as an enhancement of the low-level **thread** module. The threading module makes working with threads much easier and allows the program to run multiple operations at once.

Note that the threads in Python work best with I/O operations, such as downloading resources from the Internet or reading files and directories on your computer. If you need to do something that will be CPU intensive, then you will want to look at Python's **multiprocessing** module instead. The reason for this is that Python has the Global Interpreter Lock (GIL) that basically makes all threads run inside of one master thread. Because of this, when you go to run multiple CPU intensive operations with threads, you may find that it actually runs slower. So we will be focusing on what threads do best: I/O operations!

Intro to threads

A thread let's you run a piece of long running code as if it were a separate program. It's kind of like calling **subprocess** except that you are calling a function or class instead of a separate program. I always find it helpful to look at a concrete example. Let's take a look at something that's really simple:

```python
import threading


def doubler(number):
    """
    A function that can be used by a thread
    """
    print(threading.currentThread().getName() + '\n')
    print(number * 2)
    print()


if __name__ == '__main__':
    for i in range(5):
```

```
15          my_thread = threading.Thread(target=doubler, args=(i,))
16          my_thread.start()
```

Here we import the threading module and create a regular function called **doubler**. Our function takes a value and doubles it. It also prints out the name of the thread that is calling the function and prints a blank line at the end. Then in the last block of code, we create five threads and start each one in turn. You will note that when we instantiate a thread, we set its **target** to our doubler function and we also pass an argument to the function. The reason the **args** parameter looks a bit odd is that we need to pass a sequence to the doubler function and it only takes one argument, so we need to put a comma on the end to actually create a sequence of one.

Note that if you'd like to wait for a thread to terminate, you would need to call its **join()** method.

When you run this code, you should get the following output:

```
1   Thread-1
2
3   0
4
5   Thread-2
6
7   2
8
9   Thread-3
10
11  4
12
13  Thread-4
14
15  6
16
17  Thread-5
18
19  8
```

Of course, you normally wouldn't want to print your output to stdout. This can end up being a really jumbled mess when you do. Instead, you should use Python's **logging** module. It's thread-safe and does an excellent job. Let's modify the example above to use the logging module and name our threads while we'll at it:

```python
1   import logging
2   import threading
3
4   def get_logger():
5       logger = logging.getLogger("threading_example")
6       logger.setLevel(logging.DEBUG)
7
8       fh = logging.FileHandler("threading.log")
9       fmt = '%(asctime)s - %(threadName)s - %(levelname)s - %(message)s'
10      formatter = logging.Formatter(fmt)
11      fh.setFormatter(formatter)
12
13      logger.addHandler(fh)
14      return logger
15
16
17  def doubler(number, logger):
18      """
19      A function that can be used by a thread
20      """
21      logger.debug('doubler function executing')
22      result = number * 2
23      logger.debug('doubler function ended with: {}'.format(
24          result))
25
26
27  if __name__ == '__main__':
28      logger = get_logger()
29      thread_names = ['Mike', 'George', 'Wanda', 'Dingbat', 'Nina']
30      for i in range(5):
31          my_thread = threading.Thread(
32              target=doubler, name=thread_names[i], args=(i, logger))
33          my_thread.start()
```

The big change in this code is the addition of the **get_logger** function. This piece of code will create a logger that's set to the debug level. It will save the log to the current working directory (i.e. where the script is run from) and then we set up the format for each line logged. The format includes the time stamp, the thread name, the logging level and the message logged.

In the doubler function, we change our **print** statements to logging statements. You will note that we are passing the logger into the doubler function when we create the thread. The reason we do this is that if you instantiated the logging object in each thread, you would end up with multiple logging singletons and your log would have a lot of duplicate lines in it.

Lastly, we name our threads by creating a list of names and then setting each thread to a specific name using the **name** parameter. When you run this code, you should get a log file with the following contents:

```
1   2016-07-24 20:39:50,055 - Mike - DEBUG - doubler function executing
2   2016-07-24 20:39:50,055 - Mike - DEBUG - doubler function ended with: 0
3   2016-07-24 20:39:50,055 - George - DEBUG - doubler function executing
4   2016-07-24 20:39:50,056 - George - DEBUG - doubler function ended with: 2
5   2016-07-24 20:39:50,056 - Wanda - DEBUG - doubler function executing
6   2016-07-24 20:39:50,056 - Wanda - DEBUG - doubler function ended with: 4
7   2016-07-24 20:39:50,056 - Dingbat - DEBUG - doubler function executing
8   2016-07-24 20:39:50,057 - Dingbat - DEBUG - doubler function ended with: 6
9   2016-07-24 20:39:50,057 - Nina - DEBUG - doubler function executing
10  2016-07-24 20:39:50,057 - Nina - DEBUG - doubler function ended with: 8
```

That output is pretty self-explanatory, so let's move on. I want to cover one more topic in this section. Namely, subclassing **threading.Thread**. Let's take this last example and instead of calling Thread directly, we'll create our own custom subclass. Here is the updated code:

```
1   import logging
2   import threading
3
4   class MyThread(threading.Thread):
5
6       def __init__(self, number, logger):
7           threading.Thread.__init__(self)
8           self.number = number
9           self.logger = logger
10
11      def run(self):
12          """
13          Run the thread
14          """
15          logger.debug('Calling doubler')
16          doubler(self.number, self.logger)
17
18
19  def get_logger():
20      logger = logging.getLogger("threading_example")
21      logger.setLevel(logging.DEBUG)
22
23      fh = logging.FileHandler("threading_class.log")
```

```
24          fmt = '%(asctime)s - %(threadName)s - %(levelname)s - %(message)s'
25          formatter = logging.Formatter(fmt)
26          fh.setFormatter(formatter)
27
28          logger.addHandler(fh)
29          return logger
30
31
32  def doubler(number, logger):
33          """
34          A function that can be used by a thread
35          """
36          logger.debug('doubler function executing')
37          result = number * 2
38          logger.debug('doubler function ended with: {}'.format(
39              result))
40
41
42  if __name__ == '__main__':
43          logger = get_logger()
44          thread_names = ['Mike', 'George', 'Wanda', 'Dingbat', 'Nina']
45          for i in range(5):
46              thread = MyThread(i, logger)
47              thread.setName(thread_names[i])
48              thread.start()
```

In this example, we just subclassed **threading.Thread**. We pass in the number that we want to double and the logging object as before. But this time, we set the name of the thread differently by calling **setName** on the thread object. We still need to call **start** on each thread, but you will notice that we didn't need to define that in our subclass. When you call **start**, it will run your thread by calling the **run** method. In our class, we call the doubler function to do our processing. The output is pretty much the same except that I added an extra line of output. Go ahead and run it to see what you get.

Locks and Synchronization

When you have more than one thread, then you may find yourself needing to consider how to avoid conflicts. What I mean by this is that you may have a use case where more than one thread will need to access the same resource at the same time. If you don't think about these issues and plan accordingly, then you will end up with some issues that always happen at the worst of times and usually in production.

The solution is to use locks. A lock is provided by Python's threading module and can be held by either a single thread or no thread at all. Should a thread try to acquire a lock on a resource that is already locked, that thread will basically pause until the lock is released. Let's look at a fairly typical example of some code that doesn't have any locking functionality but that should have it added:

```python
import threading

total = 0

def update_total(amount):
    """
    Updates the total by the given amount
    """
    global total
    total += amount
    print (total)

if __name__ == '__main__':
    for i in range(10):
        my_thread = threading.Thread(
            target=update_total, args=(5,))
        my_thread.start()
```

What would make this an even more interesting example would be to add a **time.sleep** call that is of varying length. Regardless, the issue here is that one thread might call **update_total** and before it's done updating it, another thread might call it and attempt to update it too. Depending on the order of operations, the value might only get added to once.

Let's add a lock to the function. There are two ways to do this. The first way would be to use a **try/finally** as we want to ensure that the lock is always released. Here's an example:

```python
import threading

total = 0
lock = threading.Lock()

def update_total(amount):
    """
    Updates the total by the given amount
    """
    global total
    lock.acquire()
    try:
```

```
13            total += amount
14        finally:
15            lock.release()
16        print (total)
17
18 if __name__ == '__main__':
19     for i in range(10):
20         my_thread = threading.Thread(
21                target=update_total, args=(5,))
22         my_thread.start()
```

Here we just acquire the lock before we do anything else. Then we attempt to update the total and finally, we release the lock and print the current total. We can actually eliminate a lot of this boilerplate using Python's **with** statement:

```
1  import threading
2
3  total = 0
4  lock = threading.Lock()
5
6  def update_total(amount):
7      """
8      Updates the total by the given amount
9      """
10     global total
11     with lock:
12         total += amount
13     print (total)
14
15 if __name__ == '__main__':
16     for i in range(10):
17         my_thread = threading.Thread(
18                target=update_total, args=(5,))
19         my_thread.start()
```

As you can see, we no longer need the **try/finally** as the context manager that is provided by the **with** statement does all of that for us.

Of course you will also find yourself writing code where you need multiple threads accessing multiple functions. When you first start writing concurrent code, you might do something like this:

```
1   import threading
2
3   total = 0
4   lock = threading.Lock()
5
6
7   def do_something():
8       lock.acquire()
9
10      try:
11          print('Lock acquired in the do_something function')
12      finally:
13          lock.release()
14          print('Lock released in the do_something function')
15
16      return "Done doing something"
17
18  def do_something_else():
19      lock.acquire()
20
21      try:
22          print('Lock acquired in the do_something_else function')
23      finally:
24          lock.release()
25          print('Lock released in the do_something_else function')
26
27      return "Finished something else"
28
29  if __name__ == '__main__':
30      result_one = do_something()
31      result_two = do_something_else()
```

This works alright in this circumstance, but suppose you have multiple threads calling both of these functions. While one thread is running over the functions, another one could be modifying the data too and you'll end up with some incorrect results. The problem is that you might not even notice the results are wrong immediately. What's the solution? Let's try to figure that out.

A common first thought would be to add a lock around the two function calls. Let's try modifying the example above to look like the following:

```
1   import threading
2
3   total = 0
4   lock = threading.RLock()
5
6   def do_something():
7
8       with lock:
9           print('Lock acquired in the do_something function')
10      print('Lock released in the do_something function')
11
12      return "Done doing something"
13
14  def do_something_else():
15      with lock:
16          print('Lock acquired in the do_something_else function')
17      print('Lock released in the do_something_else function')
18
19      return "Finished something else"
20
21
22  def main():
23      with lock:
24          result_one = do_something()
25          result_two = do_something_else()
26
27      print (result_one)
28      print (result_two)
29
30  if __name__ == '__main__':
31      main()
```

When you actually go to run this code, you will find that it just hangs. The reason is that we just told the threading module to acquire the lock. So when we call the first function, it finds that the lock is already held and blocks. It will continue to block until the lock is released, which will never happen.

The real solution here is to use a **Re-Entrant Lock**. Python's threading module provides one via the **RLock** function. Just change the line **lock = threading.Lock()** to **lock = threading.RLock()** and try re-running the code. Your code should work now!

If you want to try the code above with actual threads, then we can replace the call to **main** with the following:

```
1   if __name__ == '__main__':
2       for i in range(10):
3           my_thread = threading.Thread(
4               target=main)
5           my_thread.start()
```

This will run the **main** function in each thread, which will in turn call the other two functions. You'll end up with 10 sets of output too.

Timers

The threading module has a neat class called **Timer** that you can use to represent an action that should take place after a specified amount of time. They actually spin up their own custom thread and are started using the same **start()** method that a regular thread uses. You can also stop a timer using its **cancel** method. It should be noted that you can even cancel the timer before it's even started.

The other day I ran into a use case where I needed to communicate with a subprocess I had started but I needed it to timeout. While there are lots of different approaches to this particular problem, my favorite solution was using the threading module's Timer class.

For this example, we will look at using the **ping** command. In Linux, the ping command will run until you kill it. So the Timer class becomes especially handy in Linux-land. Here's an example:

```
1   import subprocess
2
3   from threading import Timer
4
5   kill = lambda process: process.kill()
6   cmd = ['ping', 'www.google.com']
7   ping = subprocess.Popen(
8       cmd, stdout=subprocess.PIPE, stderr=subprocess.PIPE)
9
10  my_timer = Timer(5, kill, [ping])
11
12  try:
13      my_timer.start()
14      stdout, stderr = ping.communicate()
15  finally:
16      my_timer.cancel()
17
18  print (str(stdout))
```

Here we just set up a lambda that we can use to kill the process. Then we start our ping job and create a Timer object. You will note that the first argument is the time in seconds to wait, then the function to call and the argument to pass to the function. In this case, our function is a lambda and we pass it a list of arguments where the list happens to only have one element. If you run this code, it should run for about 5 seconds and then print out the results of the ping.

Other Thread Components

The threading module includes support for other items too. For example, you can create a **Semaphore** which is one of the oldest synchronization primitives in computer science. Basically, a Semaphore manages an internal counter which will be decremented whenever you call **acquire** on it and **incremented when you call**release*. *The counter is designed in such a way that it cannot go below zero. So if you happen to call*acquire* when it's zero, then it will block.

Another useful tool that's included is the **Event**. It will allow you to communicate between threads using signals. We will be looking at an example that uses an Event in the next section.

Finally in Python 3.2, the **Barrier** object was added. The Barrier is a primitive that basically manages a thread pool wherein the threads have to wait for each other. To pass the barrier, the thread needs to call the **wait()** method which will block until all the threads have made the call. Then it will release all the threads simultaneously.

Thread Communication

There are some use cases where you will want to have your threads communicate with each other. As we mentioned earlier, you can use create an **Event** for this purpose. But a more common method is to use a **Queue**. For our example, we'll actually use both! Let's see what that looks like:

```python
import threading

from queue import Queue


def creator(data, q):
    """
    Creates data to be consumed and waits for the consumer
    to finish processing
    """
    print('Creating data and putting it on the queue')
    for item in data:
        evt = threading.Event()
        q.put((item, evt))
```

```
15
16              print('Waiting for data to be doubled')
17              evt.wait()
18
19
20  def my_consumer(q):
21      """
22      Consumes some data and works on it
23
24      In this case, all it does is double the input
25      """
26      while True:
27          data, evt = q.get()
28          print('data found to be processed: {}'.format(data))
29          processed = data * 2
30          print(processed)
31          evt.set()
32          q.task_done()
33
34
35  if __name__ == '__main__':
36      q = Queue()
37      data = [5, 10, 13, -1]
38      thread_one = threading.Thread(target=creator, args=(data, q))
39      thread_two = threading.Thread(target=my_consumer, args=(q,))
40      thread_one.start()
41      thread_two.start()
42
43      q.join()
```

Let's break this down a bit. First off, we have a creator (AKA a producer) function that we use to create data that we want to work on (or consume). Then we have another function that we use for processing the data that we are calling **my_consumer**. The creator function will use the Queue's **put** method to put the data into the Queue and the consumer will continually check for more data and process it when it becomes available. The Queue handles all the acquires and releases of the locks so you don't have to.

In this example, we create a list of values that we want to double. Then we create two threads, one for the creator / producer and one for the consumer. You will note that we pass a Queue object to each thread which is the magic behind how the locks get handled. The queue will have the first thread feed data to the second. When the first puts some data into the queue, it also passes in an Event and then waits for the event to finish. Then in the consumer, the data is processed and when it's done, it calls the **set** method of the Event which tells the first thread that the second is done processing and it can continue.

The very last line of code call's the Queue object's **join** method which tells the Queue to wait for the threads to finish. The first thread ends when it runs out of items to put into the Queue.

Wrapping Up

We covered a lot of material here. You have learned the following:

- The basics of threading
- How locking works
- What Events are and how they can be used
- How to use a Timer
- Inter-Thread Communication using Queues / Events

Now that you know how threads are used and what they are good for, I hope you will find many good uses for them in your own code.

Chapter 29 - The multiprocessing Module

The multiprocessing module was added to Python in version 2.6. It was originally defined in PEP 371 by Jesse Noller and Richard Oudkerk. The multiprocessing module allows you to spawn processes in much that same manner than you can spawn threads with the threading module. The idea here is that because you are now spawning processes, you can avoid the Global Interpreter Lock (GIL) and take full advantages of multiple processors on a machine.

The multiprocessing package also includes some APIs that are not in the threading module at all. For example, there is a neat Pool class that you can use to parallelize executing a function across multiple inputs. We will be looking at Pool in a later section. We will start with the multiprocessing module's **Process** class.

Getting Started With Multiprocessing

The **Process** class is very similar to the threading module's Thread class. Let's try creating a series of processes that call the same function and see how that works:

```
1   import os
2
3   from multiprocessing import Process
4
5
6   def doubler(number):
7       """
8       A doubling function that can be used by a process
9       """
10      result = number * 2
11      proc = os.getpid()
12      print('{0} doubled to {1} by process id: {2}'.format(
13          number, result, proc))
14
15  if __name__ == '__main__':
```

```
16      numbers = [5, 10, 15, 20, 25]
17      procs = []
18
19      for index, number in enumerate(numbers):
20          proc = Process(target=doubler, args=(number,))
21          procs.append(proc)
22          proc.start()
23
24      for proc in procs:
25          proc.join()
```

For this example, we import Process and create a **doubler** function. Inside the function, we double the number that was passed in. We also use Python's **os** module to get the current process's ID (or pid). This will tell us which process is calling the function. Then in the block of code at the bottom, we create a series of Processes and start them. The very last loop just calls the **join()** method on each process, which tells Python to wait for the process to terminate. If you need to stop a process, you can call its **terminate()** method.

When you run this code, you should see output that is similar to the following:

```
1   5 doubled to 10 by process id: 10468
2   10 doubled to 20 by process id: 10469
3   15 doubled to 30 by process id: 10470
4   20 doubled to 40 by process id: 10471
5   25 doubled to 50 by process id: 10472
```

Sometimes it's nicer to have a more human readable name for your process though. Fortunately, the Process class does allow you to access the name of your process. Let's take a look:

```
1   import os
2
3   from multiprocessing import Process, current_process
4
5
6   def doubler(number):
7       """
8       A doubling function that can be used by a process
9       """
10      result = number * 2
11      proc_name = current_process().name
12      print('{0} doubled to {1} by: {2}'.format(
13          number, result, proc_name))
```

```
14
15
16  if __name__ == '__main__':
17      numbers = [5, 10, 15, 20, 25]
18      procs = []
19      proc = Process(target=doubler, args=(5,))
20
21      for index, number in enumerate(numbers):
22          proc = Process(target=doubler, args=(number,))
23          procs.append(proc)
24          proc.start()
25
26      proc = Process(target=doubler, name='Test', args=(2,))
27      proc.start()
28      procs.append(proc)
29
30      for proc in procs:
31          proc.join()
```

This time around, we import something extra: **current_process**. The current_process is basically the same thing as the threading module's **current_thread**. We use it to grab the name of the thread that is calling our function. You will note that for the first five processes, we don't set a name. Then for the sixth, we set the process name to "Test". Let's see what we get for output:

```
1  5 doubled to 10 by: Process-2
2  10 doubled to 20 by: Process-3
3  15 doubled to 30 by: Process-4
4  20 doubled to 40 by: Process-5
5  25 doubled to 50 by: Process-6
6  2 doubled to 4 by: Test
```

The output demonstrates that the multiprocessing module assigns a number to each process as a part of its name by default. Of course, when we specify a name, a number isn't going to get added to it.

Locks

The multiprocessing module supports locks in much the same way as the threading module does. All you need to do is import **Lock**, acquire it, do something and release it. Let's take a look:

```
1    from multiprocessing import Process, Lock
2
3
4    def printer(item, lock):
5        """
6        Prints out the item that was passed in
7        """
8        lock.acquire()
9        try:
10           print(item)
11       finally:
12           lock.release()
13
14   if __name__ == '__main__':
15       lock = Lock()
16       items = ['tango', 'foxtrot', 10]
17       for item in items:
18           p = Process(target=printer, args=(item, lock))
19           p.start()
```

Here we create a simple printing function that prints whatever you pass to it. To prevent the processes from interfering with each other, we use a Lock object. This code will loop over our list of three items and create a process for each of them. Each process will call our function and pass it one of the items from the iterable. Because we're using locks, the next process in line will wait for the lock to release before it can continue.

Logging

Logging processes is a little different than logging threads. The reason for this is that Python's logging packages doesn't use process shared locks, so it's possible for you to end up with messages from different processes getting mixed up. Let's try adding basic logging to the previous example. Here's the code:

```
1   import logging
2   import multiprocessing
3
4   from multiprocessing import Process, Lock
5
6
7   def printer(item, lock):
8       """
9       Prints out the item that was passed in
10      """
11      lock.acquire()
12      try:
13          print(item)
14      finally:
15          lock.release()
16
17  if __name__ == '__main__':
18      lock = Lock()
19      items = ['tango', 'foxtrot', 10]
20      multiprocessing.log_to_stderr()
21      logger = multiprocessing.get_logger()
22      logger.setLevel(logging.INFO)
23      for item in items:
24          p = Process(target=printer, args=(item, lock))
25          p.start()
```

The simplest way to log is to send it all to stderr. We can do this by calling the **log_to_stderr()** function. Then we call the **get_logger** function to get access to a logger and set its logging level to INFO. The rest of the code is the same. I will note that I'm not calling the **join()** method here. Instead, the parent thread (i.e. your script) will call **join()** implicitly when it exits.

When you do this, you should get output like the following:

```
1   [INFO/Process-1] child process calling self.run()
2   tango
3   [INFO/Process-1] process shutting down
4   [INFO/Process-1] process exiting with exitcode 0
5   [INFO/Process-2] child process calling self.run()
6   [INFO/MainProcess] process shutting down
7   foxtrot
8   [INFO/Process-2] process shutting down
9   [INFO/Process-3] child process calling self.run()
10  [INFO/Process-2] process exiting with exitcode 0
```

```
11   10
12   [INFO/MainProcess] calling join() for process Process-3
13   [INFO/Process-3] process shutting down
14   [INFO/Process-3] process exiting with exitcode 0
15   [INFO/MainProcess] calling join() for process Process-2
```

Let's move on and learn about Pools.

The Pool Class

The Pool class is used to represent a pool of worker processes. It has methods which can allow you to offload tasks to the worker processes. Let's look at a really simple example:

```python
1    from multiprocessing import Pool
2
3
4    def doubler(number):
5        return number * 2
6
7    if __name__ == '__main__':
8        numbers = [5, 10, 20]
9        pool = Pool(processes=3)
10       print(pool.map(doubler, numbers))
```

Basically what's happening here is that we create an instance of Pool and tell it to create three worker processes. Then we use the **map** method to map a function and an iterable to each process. Finally we print the result, which in this case is actually a list: **[10, 20, 40]**.

You can also get the result of your process in a pool by using the **apply_async** method:

```python
1    from multiprocessing import Pool
2
3
4    def doubler(number):
5        return number * 2
6
7    if __name__ == '__main__':
8        pool = Pool(processes=3)
9        result = pool.apply_async(doubler, (25,))
10       print(result.get(timeout=1))
```

What this allows us to do is actually ask for the result of the process. That is what the **get** function is all about. It tries to get our result. You will note that we also have a timeout set just in case something happened to the function we were calling. We don't want it to block indefinitely after all.

Process Communication

When it comes to communicating between processes, the multiprocessing modules has two primary methods: Queues and Pipes. The Queue implementation is actually both thread and process safe. Let's take a look at a fairly simple example that's based on the Queue code from the previous chapter:

```python
from multiprocessing import Process, Queue


sentinel = -1

def creator(data, q):
    """
    Creates data to be consumed and waits for the consumer
    to finish processing
    """
    print('Creating data and putting it on the queue')
    for item in data:

        q.put(item)


def my_consumer(q):
    """
    Consumes some data and works on it

    In this case, all it does is double the input
    """
    while True:
        data = q.get()
        print('data found to be processed: {}'.format(data))
        processed = data * 2
        print(processed)

        if data is sentinel:
            break


if __name__ == '__main__':
    q = Queue()
    data = [5, 10, 13, -1]
    process_one = Process(target=creator, args=(data, q))
```

```
37    process_two = Process(target=my_consumer, args=(q,))
38    process_one.start()
39    process_two.start()
40
41    q.close()
42    q.join_thread()
43
44    process_one.join()
45    process_two.join()
```

Here we just need to import Queue and Process. Then we two functions, one to create data and add it to the queue and the second to consume the data and process it. Adding data to the Queue is done by using the Queue's **put()** method whereas getting data from the Queue is done via the **get** method. The last chunk of code just creates the Queue object and a couple of Processes and then runs them. You will note that we call **join()** on our process objects rather than the Queue itself.

Wrapping Up

We have a lot of material here. You have learned how to use the multiprocessing module to target regular functions, communicate between processes using Queues, naming threads and much more. There is also a lot more in the Python documentation that isn't even touched in this chapter, so be sure to dive into that as well. In the meantime, you now know how to utilize all your computer's processing power with Python!

Chapter 30 - The concurrent.futures Module

The **concurrent.futures** module was added in Python 3.2. According to the Python documentation it *provides the developer with a high-level interface for asynchronously executing callables.* Basically concurrent.futures is an abstraction layer on top of Python's threading and multiprocessing modules that simplifies using them. However it should be noted that while the abstraction layer simplifies the usage of these modules, it also removes a lot of their flexibility, so if you need to do something custom, then this might not be the best module for you.

Concurrent.futures includes an abstract class called **Executor**. It cannot be used directly though, so you will need to use one of its two subclasses: **ThreadPoolExecutor** or **ProcessPoolExecutor**. As you've probably guessed, these two subclasses are mapped to Python's threading and multiprocessing APIs respectively. Both of these subclasses will provide a pool that you can put threads or processes into.

The term **future** has a special meaning in computer science. It refers to a construct that can be used for synchronization when using concurrent programming techniques. The **future** is actually a way to describe the result of a process or thread before it has finished processing. I like to think of them as a pending result.

Creating a Pool

Creating a pool of workers is extremely easy when you're using the concurrent.futures module. Let's start out by rewriting our downloading code from the **asyncio** chapter so that it now uses the concurrent.futures module. Here's my version:

```python
1   import os
2   import urllib.request
3
4   from concurrent.futures import ThreadPoolExecutor
5   from concurrent.futures import as_completed
6
7
8   def downloader(url):
9       """
10      Downloads the specified URL and saves it to disk
11      """
12      req = urllib.request.urlopen(url)
13      filename = os.path.basename(url)
14      ext = os.path.splitext(url)[1]
15      if not ext:
16          raise RuntimeError('URL does not contain an extension')
17
18      with open(filename, 'wb') as file_handle:
19          while True:
20              chunk = req.read(1024)
21              if not chunk:
22                  break
23              file_handle.write(chunk)
24      msg = 'Finished downloading {filename}'.format(filename=filename)
25      return msg
26
27
28  def main(urls):
29      """
30      Create a thread pool and download specified urls
31      """
32      with ThreadPoolExecutor(max_workers=5) as executor:
33          futures = [executor.submit(downloader, url) for url in urls]
34          for future in as_completed(futures):
35              print(future.result())
36
37  if __name__ == '__main__':
38      urls = ["http://www.irs.gov/pub/irs-pdf/f1040.pdf",
39              "http://www.irs.gov/pub/irs-pdf/f1040a.pdf",
40              "http://www.irs.gov/pub/irs-pdf/f1040ez.pdf",
41              "http://www.irs.gov/pub/irs-pdf/f1040es.pdf",
42              "http://www.irs.gov/pub/irs-pdf/f1040sb.pdf"]
```

```
43     main(urls)
```

First off we do the imports that we need. Then we create our **downloader** function. I went ahead and updated it slightly so it checks to see if the URL has an extension on the end of it. If it doesn't, then we'll raise a **RuntimeError**. Next we create a **main** function, which is where the thread pool gets instantiated. You can actually use Python's **with** statement with the ThreadPoolExecutor and the ProcessPoolExecutor, which is pretty handy.

Anyway, we set our pool so that it has five workers. Then we use a list comprehension to create a group of futures (or jobs) and finally we call the **as_complete** function. This handy function is an iterator that yields the futures as they complete. When they complete, we print out the result, which is a string that was returned from our downloader function.

If the function we were using was very computation intensive, then we could easily swap out ThreadPoolExecutor for ProcessPoolExecutor and only have a one line code change.

We can clean this code up a bit by using the concurrent.future's **map** method. Let's rewrite our pool code slightly to take advantage of this:

```python
1   import os
2   import urllib.request
3
4   from concurrent.futures import ThreadPoolExecutor
5   from concurrent.futures import as_completed
6
7
8   def downloader(url):
9       """
10      Downloads the specified URL and saves it to disk
11      """
12      req = urllib.request.urlopen(url)
13      filename = os.path.basename(url)
14      ext = os.path.splitext(url)[1]
15      if not ext:
16          raise RuntimeError('URL does not contain an extension')
17
18      with open(filename, 'wb') as file_handle:
19          while True:
20              chunk = req.read(1024)
21              if not chunk:
22                  break
23              file_handle.write(chunk)
24      msg = 'Finished downloading {filename}'.format(filename=filename)
25      return msg
```

```
26
27
28   def main(urls):
29       """
30       Create a thread pool and download specified urls
31       """
32       with ThreadPoolExecutor(max_workers=5) as executor:
33           return executor.map(downloader, urls, timeout=60)
34
35   if __name__ == '__main__':
36       urls = ["http://www.irs.gov/pub/irs-pdf/f1040.pdf",
37               "http://www.irs.gov/pub/irs-pdf/f1040a.pdf",
38               "http://www.irs.gov/pub/irs-pdf/f1040ez.pdf",
39               "http://www.irs.gov/pub/irs-pdf/f1040es.pdf",
40               "http://www.irs.gov/pub/irs-pdf/f1040sb.pdf"]
41       results = main(urls)
42       for result in results:
43           print(result)
```

The primary difference here is in the **main** function, which has been reduced by two lines of code. The *map** method is just like Python's map in that it takes a function and an iterable and then calls the function for each item in the iterable. You can also add a timeout for each of your threads so that if one of them hangs, it will get stopped. Lastly, starting in Python 3.5, they added a **chunksize** argument, which can help performance when using the Thread pool when you have a very large iterable. However if you happen to be using the Process pool, the chunksize will have no effect.

Deadlocks

One of the pitfalls to the concurrent.futures module is that you can accidentally create deadlocks when the caller to associate with a **Future** is also waiting on the results of another future. This sounds kind of confusing, so let's look at an example:

```
1   from concurrent.futures import ThreadPoolExecutor
2
3
4   def wait_forever():
5       """
6       This function will wait forever if there's only one
7       thread assigned to the pool
8       """
9       my_future = executor.submit(zip, [1, 2, 3], [4, 5, 6])
```

```
10        result = my_future.result()
11        print(result)
12
13    if __name__ == '__main__':
14        executor = ThreadPoolExecutor(max_workers=1)
15        executor.submit(wait_forever)
```

Here we import the ThreadPoolExecutor class and create an instance of it. Take note that we set its maximum number of workers to one thread. Then we submit our function, **wait_forever**. Inside of our function, we submit another job to the thread pool that is supposed to zip two lists together, get the result of that operation and print it out. However we've just created a deadlock! The reason is that we are having one Future wait for another Future to finish. Basically we want a pending operation to wait on another pending operation which doesn't work very well.

Let's rewrite the code a bit to make it work:

```
1    from concurrent.futures import ThreadPoolExecutor
2
3
4    def wait_forever():
5        """
6        This function will wait forever if there's only one
7        thread assigned to the pool
8        """
9        my_future = executor.submit(zip, [1, 2, 3], [4, 5, 6])
10
11       return my_future
12
13   if __name__ == '__main__':
14       executor = ThreadPoolExecutor(max_workers=3)
15       fut = executor.submit(wait_forever)
16
17       result = fut.result()
18       print(list(result.result()))
```

In this case, we just return the inner future from the function and then ask for its result. The result of calling **result** on our returned future is another future that actually contains the result we want, which is a bit confusing. Anyway, if we call the **result** method on this nested future, we get a **zip** object back, so to find out what the actual result is, we wrap the zip with Python's **list** function and print it out.

Wrapping Up

Now you have another neat concurrency tool to use. You can easily create thread or process pools depending on your needs. Should you need to run a process that is network or I/O bound, you can use the thread pool class. If you have a computationally heavy task, then you'll want to use the process pool class instead. Just be careful of calling futures incorrectly or you might get a deadlock.